Start Your Own

BLOGGING BUSINESS

Additional titles in *Entrepreneur's **Startup Series***

Start Your Own

Bar and Tavern

Bed & Breakfast

Business on eBay

Business Support Service

Car Wash

Child-Care Service

Cleaning Service

Clothing Store

Consulting

Crafts Business

e-Business

e-Learning Business

Event Planning Business

Executive Recruiting Service

Freight Brokerage Business

Gift Basket Service

Growing and Selling Herbs and Herbal
  Products

Home Inspection Service

Import/Export Business

Information Consultant Business

Law Practice

Lawn Care Business

Mail Order Business

Medical Claims Billing Service

Personal Concierge Service

Personal Training Business

Pet-Sitting Business

Restaurant and Five Other Food Businesses

Self-Publishing Business

Seminar Production Business

Specialty Travel & Tour Business

Staffing Service

Successful Retail Business

Vending Business

Wedding Consultant Business

Wholesale Distribution Business

Entrepreneur
MAGAZINE'S

start up

Start Your Own

BLOGGING BUSINESS

Generate Income from Advertisers, Subscribers, Merchandising and More

Entrepreneur Press and J. S. McDougall

EP
Entrepreneur
Press

Editorial Director: Jere L. Calmes
Managing Editor: Marla Markman
Cover Design: Beth Hansen-Winter
Production and Composition: Eliot House Productions

This publication is designed to provide accurate and authoritative information in regard to the subject matter covered. It is sold with the understanding that the publisher is not engaged in rendering legal, accounting or other professional services. If legal advice or other expert assistance is required, the services of a competent professional person should be sought.

Library of Congress Cataloging-in-Publication Data
McDougall, J. S.
    Start your own blogging business/by Entrepreneur Press and J. S. McDougall.
        p.   cm.
    ISBN 978-1-59918-047-2 (alk. paper)
    ISBN 1-59918-047-2 (alk. paper)
        1. Blogs. 2. Web site development—Amateurs' manuals. 3. Blogs—Economic aspects. I. Entrepreneur Press. II. Title.
    TK5105.8884.M33 2007
    070.5'7973—dc22   2006011748

Printed in Canada

12 11 10 09   10 9 8 7 6 5 4

Contents

▲

Preface

As recently as ten years ago, blogs didn't exist. The internet itself was still in its infant stages and was populated mostly by academic research papers and shrines to Jennifer Aniston. The blogs that you hear about today in every newspaper, television program, and magazine article had yet to explode into internet and national prominence.

Today, blogs are ubiquitous. They are influencing consumer trends, politics, journalism, and even the larger national dialogue. At their most basic level, blogs seem rather benign. Put simply, a blog is nothing more than a web site that publishes new material at regular periodic intervals—often several times a day. The reason this new publishing format has become so powerful has little to do with the actual format at all. The power of blogs is rooted in their ability to enable billions of average people to publish content that is instantly accessible around the globe. When coupled with the rapid-fire publishing schedule that many blogs maintain, this new way of publishing enables news, thoughts, opinions, and other content to spread around the world in a matter of minutes. Old-style content publishers are having a difficult time keeping up.

Fifty-seven million American adults read blogs. That is 39 percent of all internet users in this country. This is a startling percentage made even more startling when one takes into consideration that a few years ago nobody knew what a blog was. The popularity of blogs as a viable form of communication and publishing is exploding. In just a few years from now, 57 million readers will seem like a slow day at the office for the blogosphere.

Blogging is being embraced by artists, politicians, corporations, and hobbyists as one of the fastest and most effective forms of communication available today. For example, in lieu of publishing a quarterly newsletter some companies now publish a daily blog. Instead of soliciting agents and editors and publishers, artists are finding it easier to reach their audiences directly through the use of a blog. Idle teenagers, aging grandmothers, even ambitious pets are signing on to the blogosphere to make their voices heard.

As eyes turn away from television screens, magazines, and newspapers to the daily content produced by bloggers, commercial opportunities follow. Blogs by nature have specific subjects with specific audiences. Advertisers have recognized this new and exciting opportunity and are sinking mountains of cash into blog advertising because it is highly targeted, effective, and entirely measurable.

The blogging revolution marks an exciting turning point in the history of publishing, and the brief history of the internet. For the first time in history, it is not only possible, but also simple and cheap, to publish content instantly in a manner that is accessible anywhere on the planet. Anybody able to put together interesting, quality content on a consistent basis now has the ability to rub elbows with *GQ*, *The Boston Globe*, and *MacAddict*. Many small blogs with hot topics that began as the thoughts of one lone blogger (Engadget, DailyKOS, PinkIsTheNewBlog, etc.) have taken off to earn hundreds of thousands of dollars per year in advertising, merchandising, and memberships.

Let's take a look at a hypothetical blogging business. Example blogger, Caroline, publishes a blog about her favorite things in the world: Apple's iPods. Every day on the blog Caroline publishes several posts containing content such as reviews of the latest iPods, tips on how to get the most out of iPods, tweaks on how to modify iPods, and reviews of all the latest iPod accessories. Fellow iPod devotees pour over Caroline's blog regularly for the exciting new information she provides.

Her blog receives, on average, 15,000 visitors per day—a modest amount of traffic given her chosen topic. Along the side of Caroline's blog, she has placed sponsored advertisements where dealers of the iPod and iPod accessories have agreed to pay her between $.80 and $1 (a normal rate for such an in-demand item) every time a reader clicks on their advertisement. If only 150 people (only 1 percent of her daily traffic) click on any advertisement in a day, Caroline has earned between $120 and $150—just for writing about her favorite topic.

If Caroline is able to sustain 150 clicks per day for a month, she'll earn $4,500 in one month, or $54,000 per year. That's a sizable income! Now, if Caroline is able to increase her traffic from 15,000 to 150,000 per day, while maintaining her 1 percent click-rate, she'll bring in $1,500 per day, or just over a half million dollars per year.

As you can see, blogging as a business is not a radical idea. Any publication, whether it is print, audio, video, or even skywriting, can bring in money if it brings in an audience. This book will help readers recognize and capitalize on the immense opportunity that awaits any person with passion, patience, and a PC. Blogging has overcome its "talkative-geek-in-the-basement-behind-a-computer" stereotype. It is now a viable and accepted form of mass publication. And due to its low cost of entry, the simple blogging tools now available, and the massive reach of the internet, anybody can build a profitable business publishing blogs.

*This book is dedicated to Jack
for his help in starting a career.*

1

Planning
Your Blog

Blogging is the internet's newest surprise. Just when it appeared that the 'net was on track for exclusive corporate commercialization, blogging came along and detoured the whole hurtling freight train of money. Many consider this new phenomenon of blogging to be the Great Equalizer. Creative and considerate and charismatic people are now able

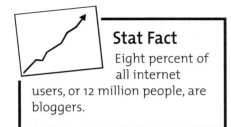

Stat Fact
Eight percent of all internet users, or 12 million people, are bloggers.

to bypass the usual corporate content publishers—such as magazine editors, music labels, television executives—and deliver work directly to their awaiting audiences.

If you haven't allowed yourself to wander beyond your usual favorite web sites, you'll be surprised to find that the number of online journals, photo albums, music galleries, artist portfolios, and other personal sites have exploded in number. Thousands of people every day are discovering services and applications that make it easy to publish and distribute their creativity. As a result, new and original content is flooding the web, and creating an internet renaissance.

This book will help you understand the significance of the blogging phenomenon, and show you how people around the world are using blogging to cast off commonly accepted publishing procedures and keep the profits of their own work. It will show you how to follow the same path.

The material presented is designed around a three-step process, which is called the three "P"s:

Step 1: **P**lanning your Blog

Step 2: **P**ublishing your Blog

Step 3: **P**rofiting from your Blog

Three chapters of this book detail what's involved in each step of the process. All the steps are important and must be given proper time and consideration. The urge to publish your work can be hard to resist—as can the urge to begin collecting profits—but rushing through the early planning stages can leave you stranded down the road. As with any business, success is impossible without a solid foundation. Take your time with each step.

There's no limit to how much money you can earn running a successful and popular blog, and this book will get you started down that path. Blogging is not, however, a get-rich-quick miracle. Self-publishing and self-promoting any type of work can be a bit like running through a gauntlet. You will get bruised and battered along the way, but you'll come out better off for it on the other side. You will need to put in serious work, not only on your chosen craft, whether it is writing, photography, cartooning, or anything else, but also on the less appealing business side of your endeavor.

Once you begin collecting money, either from your audience or your advertisers, people will come to depend on you as they would on any other business. You will need to handle actual paperwork, put in long hours at the keyboard,

Tip...

Smart Tip
Plan early for proper financial practices. Line up any help you will need now so that when the money starts to come in, you will be ready.

and learn a thing or two about tax forms, all while providing quality and reliable content to your audience.

Tough though it may be, if you're ready and committed to begin turning a profit from your blog, there's more reward to be had than simply the profits. You can work in your underwear, feet from your bed. You never need to sit in a cubicle, and you can take six hours for lunch if you wish. Owning your schedule is its own reward.

What Is a Blog?

Before we can tackle the business of making money from a blog, we should define the scope of blogs as best we can. The term "blog" comes from the words "web log," which was used for a short time to describe web sites that published a running archive of dated entries. "Web log" quickly mushed into one word, "weblog," and in turn quickly morphed into "blog," which has been with us ever since. The word "blog," as a noun, can describe a regularly updated web site with dated posts. The word can also be used as a verb, as in "to blog," meaning to submit posts to a web site. People who run blogs are known as "bloggers," and the whole collection of all the internet's blogs is known as the "blogosphere." And a personal favorite, when veteran bloggers post an exciting entry, they often exclaim, "that's blogtastic!" Okay, I made that last one up. But the point is that the practice of blogging is evolving so rapidly that even the terms people use to describe the phenomenon are still being invented. Who knows . . . "blogtastic" might catch on.

The anatomy of a blog is nothing more than a web site with dated entries. This encompasses everything from the most common blog format of an online daily journal to up-to-the-minute news posts and more. With the recent emergence of photo blogs, video blogs, cartoon blogs, and such, the definition of blog is expanding every day.

A blog serves no single purpose. The motivations for starting a blog are as varied as the people who start them. Some people use their blogs to filter the media bombardment that our homes and cars and phones receive every day. By routing through the media din and selecting the most relevant and insightful stories, bloggers can provide a valuable service. Other bloggers use their blogs to inform like-minded hobbyists about a particular industry. For example, the lion's share of blogs on the internet are about the internet—how to build sites, what technologies to try, and what coming trends to watch. These bloggers alert their audience to exciting news by keeping a constant finger on the pulse of a particular pastime, and in that way, provide another valuable service. Bloggers even publish their

Stat Fact
Currently over 57 million American adults read blogs regularly.

> ⚠ **Beware!**
> A blog can be about anything, but to be successful, a blog must provide a valuable and tangible service to its readers.

blogs with the simple intention of making people laugh. Plenty of bloggers post cartoons, funny pictures, charming stories, and many other things that they, and their readers, find enjoyable. This, too, is a valuable service. Even big companies such as Google and Microsoft are trying to put on a friendly face by publishing blogs of their own. For little investment these companies gain the benefits of this intimate and direct medium through which to communicate with their customers. Isn't that blogtastic?

Not all blogs provide a valuable service. Some, you will find as you explore, are rambling, incoherent, and unentertaining rants about something as uninteresting as the state of the molded cheese in the blogger's mini-fridge. This type of blog has no audience beyond the blogger's mother, bless her heart. You should be certain that your blog, and your chosen topic, provides a service. If you are able to provide a valuable and reliable service of any kind, you will develop an audience. We cover more about selecting a topic for your blog later in this chapter.

Blogging is a growing, yet young, phenomenon. As blogging grows, so does your potential audience. And as more individuals and companies and organizations use blogs to communicate, more people will devote more of their time to reading the blogs that interest them. Blogging will grow to new heights in the next few years, and you are in a great position to catch the wave as it builds.

With your enthusiasm to explore the world of professional blogging, and the tools and information provided in the following chapters, you will be able to earn money running a blog. The amount of money you earn will be up to you.

The Requirements

The most important step to launching a successful blog is the planning; the first "P" in our three-step process. You must map out your plan for profitability before you begin. You wouldn't launch a business without a business plan, or a bakery without dough, or a horse stable without manure forks. This section covers the things you'll need to anticipate, and the preparations you'll need to make before ever touching your keyboard.

A profitable blog must have three main features:

1. a steady stream of content
2. a large audience
3. a reliable revenue source

You are best able to prepare for attaining these three things in the planning stages. Once you begin writing the blog, you'll have too many other concerns taking up your time to tackle planning effectively, and you may well already be committed to a path that isn't quite right for you.

Choosing a Profitable Topic

There are many factors to consider when selecting a topic that will produce desirable profits for you. You must consider public interest, your knowledge of the topic, the longevity of the topic, and more. Brainstorm several possible topics that you might like to use and test them against the following factors. A winning topic will hold up in each case. Try not to rationalize for your favorite when testing your topics. A blog about the life and times of your cat may sound fun to you, but will likely not hold the public's interest.

Interest of the General Public

The topic you select should have mass appeal of some kind. Your goal is to attract millions of visitors every month, and therefore blogging about provincial or tiny niche topics may not serve you well. For example, a blog that addresses the political happenings in your town of 30,000 people may very well become the hottest thing in town, but the audience topic has a ceiling. Realistically, it is likely that only one out of every ten people in your town have the time or interest to read blogs in the course of a day, and of those few people even less are interested in town politics. So while it may excite you personally, the reality is that this topic is limited. Here are some general topic areas to consider.

Industry Blogs

What holds a national interest and has held it for a long time? A blog about Lindsay Lohan may not be a bad idea. She's a household name. She holds people's interest. But consider what happens when she fades from the limelight and leaves your blog without new content. What then? So think bigger again. The larger topic of celebrity antics in the show business industry isn't going anywhere. As long as Hollywood continues to produce bold, beautiful people for us to gawk at, your blog will have fodder.

> **Tip...**
>
> **Smart Tip**
> Blogs about commodity items, such as digital cameras and MP3 players provide more advertising options for bloggers, and often more advertising revenue.

> **Beware!**
> Choosing a subject with too narrow a focus will limit your blog and lose the interest of your readers.

So celebrities aren't your thing. Mine either. Luckily there are thousands of possible industries that already have millions of fans. Begin by thinking about general topics such as sports, technology, fashion, or food. Then whittle your idea down to a more specific, yet massively appealing, point. The sports industry, for example, would be too large a topic to cover. People interested in NASCAR won't be interested in your bowling postings. Say basketball is your favorite sport, cover the NBA. The NBA has millions of fans, and you could produce great traffic by covering the stories that major media passes over.

If you choose to cover the technology industry, you'll quickly find that you have some significant competition. The majority of blogs on the internet are devoted to some aspect of the tech industry. Do some research before you launch your blog in this topic. Find out what's out there and find a way to do it better, or a different niche to cover. Is dissecting electronics your hobby? What about installing Linux on everything you can get your hands on? There are plenty of fan niches within the tech industry that you can certainly find a place to squeeze in.

Think about the major industries in this country. Certainly there is one that appeals to you most. If you think you can spend your days searching for industry news, industry breakthroughs, and industry gossip, you can build a blog and fan base by posting what you find.

Organization Blogs

If you have a connection to, or are employed by a company that holds national interest, such as eBay or Apple or Martha Stewart's Omnimedia, you could do well by simply discussing the antics in your office on your blog. People are always interested to hear about the inner workings of the companies that have reached celebrity status in this country. There are many successful blogs run by folks who capitalize on their company's celebrity.

Are you part of a well-known national organization such as the American Cancer Society or the National Center for Open Source Policy and Research or even Project Save-a-Puppy? If so, then there are already millions of people who are interested in the work you're involved in every day. Often large organizations cannot spend the money or the time publishing details

> **Beware!**
> Be careful not to reveal sensitive information, or bad-mouth your boss (too much). Remember blogs are public, and many people have been canned in a hurry when a 'net surfing higher-up stumbled onto something they didn't like.

of the work they do every day. By posting updates on the legislation or breakthroughs or problems facing your organization you can connect instantly with millions of readers while doing your organization the service of communicating with supporters.

Beware!
Creating a blog about your art means that you will need to consistently create art to post something new every day. This can be difficult or impossible for many artists.

Personal Blogs

Don't discount less specific blog topics, such as humor. Many successful bloggers don't cover one specific topic at all, but rather they cover a variety of topics in an entertaining manner. Think, for example, of Dave Barry's syndicated column. He doesn't restrict his writing to one area of interest, he writes about anything that flies into his head—but he does so in such a humorous way that he has achieved mass appeal. If you are good at making people laugh, go ahead and try your hand at a humor blog. If you can post something that makes people laugh every day, they'll take time out of their day to read your blog.

Posting personal artwork, such as cartoons or photography, has helped some bloggers not only earn some money from art sales or merchandising, but also gain some fans of their work. A community may begin to grow around your art, and as long as you are able to produce your art at the level that your fans have come to expect, you'll have a dedicated and reliable fan base from which to grow. A popular art blog can lead to larger licensing or merchandising or sponsorship deals.

Another neat idea which has been successful for a few bloggers is to attempt to pull off, and chronicle, something remarkable. Think of it as an on-going publicity stunt. Would you like to ride your lawnmower across the nation? Perhaps you would like to try to get a date with a famous celebrity. What about that old kayak in the shed—think it can make it to Hawaii? If this sounds like fun to you, be sure to give yourself a lot of time to ramp up publicity for your stunt before you take off. You can draw a lot of traffic in the weeks and months leading up to whatever it is you choose to pull off, but little after. Also, once you've succeeded or failed at your mission, what's next?

Beware!
Political blogs can be emotionally charged. This can make them dangerous. You might like to protect yourself and your identity if you feel like your blog might upset your family, co-workers, boss, or community.

Political Blogs

Political blogs of all persuasions exist in abundance across the internet. Second to technology, it is the most prevalent topic in the blogosphere. Joining the ranks of the would-be pundits may only be worth attempting if you can bring some credibility to the

7

effort. Everybody has an opinion on the matters of the day. Not everybody has an informed and insightful opinion.

If you would like to run a political blog, but not assert your personal opinion, you could consider using your blog as a filter to help readers wade through all the political spin. Many successful political bloggers put their egos aside and use their blog to post links to worthwhile media reports, insightful commentary, and even to other blogs. Once you establish yourself as a talented and valuable filter of the media barrage, like-minded people will visit you for their daily political news dose.

General Interest Blogs

Don't limit yourself to the topic areas listed above. There are thousands of possibilities that have yet to be explored. One never knows what will catch on and spark the interest of millions of people, especially with the wildfire-pace that word-of-mouth can travel across the internet. If you have a crazy idea that might just work, go ahead and give it a shot. The cost of entry can be so low in blogging that you've got little to lose.

Continuous Stream of Content

As the Lindsay Lohan blog example illustrated above, you need to choose a blog topic that won't dry up. Public interest is fickle and rarely stays on one topic for very long. So be sure to choose a topic that has not only held public interest for a long time, but will do so into the future.

For example, the Winter Olympics is an event that sends the whole world rushing to media outlets for the latest news, and a blog seems perfectly suited to provide up-to-the-minute updates and compelling stories about the competitors. But what do you cover after closing ceremonies and then for the next three years? Your blog will sit dormant and unprofitable while the public's interest moves on.

Let's say you're an avid gamer and are a particular fan of Microsoft's XBox 360. Instead of starting a blog about gaming on the XBox 360, consider starting a blog about gaming in general. Gaming will be around forever; the XBox 360 will eventually be replaced, leaving your blog without its star.

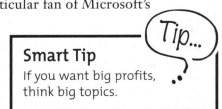

Smart Tip

If you want big profits, think big topics.

No one can control public interest. But it can be somewhat predictable. Examine trends in the past, stick to reliable topics, and don't select a subject so esoteric that you limit your own audience.

Blogger Credibility

You must have, or develop, a better-than-average familiarity with your chosen topic for readers to take you seriously. Readers won't stick around to read things they already know. You must provide them with the service of your expertise on the subject.

Therefore, you shouldn't choose a topic that you know little or nothing about. First of all, learning about your topic as you go will alienate your initial, interested audience and you'll likely develop an early stigma among the people you need most. Second, chances are that if you know nothing about it now, you don't have much interest in the subject and your current passion for the topic will wane, leaving you with a blog you can't stand. Choose a hobby of yours. If you're not an expert in any particular field now, pick an area of interest to you and buy a few books. Once you have gotten through a few, you'll likely be more well read on the topic than most of the casual hobbyists out there.

To establish credibility, you will have to choose a topic that isn't so large that your expertise is not plausible. Few people will ever be considered experts on the gigantic topic of "sports," but it is certainly possible for you to be considered an expert on the NBA. Likewise, it is doubtful that any one person will be considered an expert on "animals." It is more believable that someone is an expert on "training dogs." Choose a topic of manageable size.

Existing Competition

Before you take on all comers, find out who they are and how many of them exist. You will do yourself a disservice by entering a topic area that's already chock-full of bloggers. Similarly, taking on established field experts can be a prohibitively difficult arrangement. You shouldn't completely disregard your chosen topic if you find that it is crowded or well-covered. While that may be what you end up doing, you should consider adjusting your tactics first.

If your preferred topic is crowded, readership for that type of blog will be spread too thin across too many blogs, thereby leaving all bloggers with little traffic and little profits.

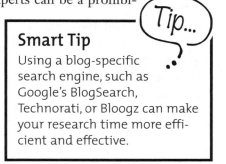

Smart Tip
Using a blog-specific search engine, such as Google's BlogSearch, Technorati, or Bloogz can make your research time more efficient and effective.

Entering this arena just to publish more of the same would be a mistake. Instead you should study your competition. Make notes of where people are succeeding and where they are falling behind. Copy what works and improve on what doesn't. Learn from your competitions' mistakes. Then, if you are able to formulate a new approach to the topic, or cover it in a new and entertaining manner, it is possi-

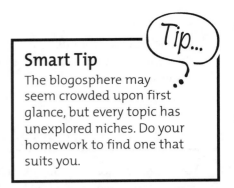

Smart Tip
The blogosphere may seem crowded upon first glance, but every topic has unexplored niches. Do your homework to find one that suits you.

ble that you could attract traffic away from each of the lackluster blogs, create sufficient traffic for your blog, and succeed in bringing cohesion to the once fragmented topic.

If you find that your topic is well-covered by a well-known expert in the field, it may be wise to decide that there's nothing more you can add and choose another topic. There are plenty out there and you can certainly find a slimmer niche to slide into. Though after reading and studying the expert's blog, if you see that there is something that you can add to the subject, or a more entertaining approach you can take, it may be worth a shot.

Your Interest

Before committing yourself to one particular topic, stop to realize that whatever topic you choose will become a focal point of every day. Your interest and passion for the topic should be strong enough to sustain you through the times when you aren't sure you can bring yourself to read another article on the subject.

Consider this fact carefully and objectively. You don't want to be stuck in a year with a blog that you can't stand and a job that you hate. Remember, you are starting a blogging business to escape jobs you hate, not to create them!

Selecting a Blog Name

Selecting a suitable name for your blog, or a pseudonym for yourself, is one of the creative parts of getting started. This is where you get to put your razor-sharp wit to good use. Naming your blog is necessary, of course. It will be how people find and recognize you. Inventing a pseudonym for yourself, however, is optional, but can be just as fun.

When naming your blog, there are a few guidelines you should follow. First, create a descriptive name that is appropriate for your blog topic. Let's say a blogger named Alex decides to use the simple name of "Alex's Blog." While this title is accurate, it doesn't give readers any indication as to what Alex's blog is about. A blog name should tell readers how they will benefit from coming to the blog. The title of "Alex's Cute Dog Photo Blog" makes clear that Alex's blog offers photos of cute dogs. Readers looking to brighten their day with adorable photos will know where to come.

Domain Name Concerns

Keep your site's domain name in mind when naming your blog. Ideally, your blog's name should be your blog's domain name to keep things simple for your readers. Therefore, you should choose a brief, memorable name that works well with ".com" tagged on the end of it. If Alex were to name his site "Alex's Archive of Adorable Puppy Photography," the sheer length of the name alone could easily overwhelm the constraints of a suitable domain name. The URL, alexsarchiveofadorablepuppyphotography.com, isn't exactly a treat to type, let alone remember. Shortening the name to "Cute K-9 Blog" would work better. The URL, cuteK9blog.com, is memorable, brief, easy to spell, and appropriate for the subject matter.

Whatever you end up choosing, expect it to be permanent. Changing the name of your blog will not only confuse your readers and harm your established brand credibility, but it will wreak havoc on any links you have strewn around the blogosphere. If readers expect a link will take them to "Alex's Blog," but they end up at "Cute K-9 Blog," they'll think an error has occurred and will likely leave your site. Also, search engines will take a while to catch up to the switch, if they manage to at all. It is unlikely that searches for the established "Alex's Blog" will send people to the new "Cute K-9 Blog" without some fancy keyword shenanigans on Alex's part.

Choosing a Pseudonym

Choosing a pseudonym for yourself isn't necessary, but many bloggers choose to do so either for the added layer of online protection from online evil, or for the plain fun of it. Who wouldn't want to create an online alter-ego? The sky's the limit when renaming yourself. The only advice we can offer is to avoid choosing anything inappropriate or offensive. You wouldn't want to alienate some potential readers of your dessert recipe blog just because you wanted to name yourself BigHairyToe.

▲

Tip...

Smart Tip

Set up a separate e-mail address for your blog that is different from your personal e-mail address. This will help guard your personal address from SPAM, stalkers, and the other security hazards of public e-mail addressses.

There are significant drawbacks to using your real name. First, if you run a blog that feeds off any aspect of your personal life, you run the risk of revealing too much and making yourself vulnerable to identity thieves. Second, if you write any sort of highly opinionated or "questionable" material, you may be shooting yourself in the foot when applying for your next job, beginning a new relationship, or even applying to schools. It's no secret that people often search the internet for the names of prospective employees, dates, and school applicants. If they come across your blog and read something that concerns them, you could be passed over.

To protect your anonymity, consider creating an online alter ego named "Captain Fido, Lord of all Dog Photographers." Or, why not just become "Mr. Blogtastic"? The benefits of keeping your personal and professional blogging career separate could be worth it.

If you aren't publishing highly opinionated or questionable material on your blog and just seek to provide a valuable, thoughtful service for readers, using your real name could be a good move. If you're trying to establish yourself as an expert in your chosen field, a pseudonym could hinder your progress. Media outlets, book publishers, and magazine editors are slower to call "Captain Fido" for his thoughts than they are to call a real person.

Choosing a Platform for Growth

Now that the intangibles are out of the way, it's time to start planning the logistical aspects of getting your blog up and running. There are countless options when it comes to blog software or services, and to cover them all in one book is not plausible. Chapter 2 covers the most popular blogging options. First, here is an overview of the blogging software landscape and some tips on what to seek out, and what to avoid, in blog software.

Hosted Blogging Service *vs.* Installed Server Application

There are two main types of blogging platforms: hosted service and server application. Both perform basically the same task of publishing a blog. Any, of either type,

Dollar Stretcher

There are many quality free hosted blogging services, so if you're looking to save money at the outset, this is a good way to go.

will meet your needs, and unless you go with an early version of some new application, all have been around long enough that the bugs have been worked out.

There are significant technological differences between hosted blogging services and installed server applications. The method you choose will have significant effects on how you run your blog.

Hosted Blogging Service

A hosted blogging service is an entirely web-based service like Gmail or PayPal. All your interactions with the blogging service, including setting up and posting to your own blog, are done through the blogging service's web site. There is nothing to download, nothing to install, and you can begin blogging immediately. (Some blogging services do have helper applications that you can download by choice if you want to submit posts from a desktop application, but it isn't necessary.)

You will need to register for the blogging service by providing at least your name and e-mail address. Once registered, you are given a web address location for your blog. Your blog's address, at least initially, will be some extension of the blogging service's address. Some services allow you to choose this extension and some assign it to you. Your new blog's address could take the format of any of the examples below.

Assigned: www.blogservices.com/12d123dksa9

Chosen: www.blogservices.com/cuteK9blog

Chosen: http://cuteK9blog.blogservices.com

For casual bloggers, the provided address will usually suffice. Though if your goal is big traffic (and whose isn't?) you should invest in your own personal domain name and configure it to redirect to the address assigned to you by the blogging service. A domain name registrar such as GoDaddy.com or Enom.com can help you register and redirect a domain. The benefit of this strategy is that you can advertise your own, easy-to-remember and more professional domain name, which would automatically redirect your visitors to your blog. For example, when a visitor types your newly registered domain name into their browser (www.cuteK9blog.com) your domain registrar service (such as GoDaddy or Enom) will forward that visitor automatically to the actual home of your blog. The advantage to this method is that by using your own domain name, you can have a neat .com that is easy to remember, which automatically redirects visitors to the less friendly, often confusing, address given to your blog by the blogging service.

VISITOR —> www.cuteK9blog.com —> www.blogservices.com/12d123dksa9

Dollar Stretcher

Most domain name registrars offer a discount on registration fees if you purchase more than one year at a time. If you're sure you would like the selected domain for a while, buy some years up front to save some money.

Blogging services have multiple levels of service, ranging from a basic free service to a more expensive, fully featured service. As your blog outgrows the basic level of service, your fees will increase. The good news is that the top-level of service isn't very expensive; services range from $15 to $30 per month. Hopefully, you'll be able to cover that cost in revenue within a few months of launch.

The disadvantage to hosted blogging services is the limited ability to customize your site. Some places do allow quite a bit, but complete customization isn't possible as you won't have access to much of the code of your web site. Therefore, in places, you'll be forced to shoehorn your blog into the service's mold.

Also, if you use a hosted blogging service and their servers go down for any amount of time, you're left largely without recourse. You'll have to wait it out with the rest of the bloggers on the system. If you sign on with an established and reputable service, this shouldn't be a large concern for you, as they no doubt have a robust network and highly-skilled technicians. But if you hosted your own blogging application or used a separate web host, you could take a more active role in getting the site back online.

Another drawback of hosted blogging services is that your blog will be on a server with thousands of other blogs. Your site is at the mercy of the other bloggers on the service. You will never know what other blogs are on the same server with yours, or how many. If one of those blogs has a huge traffic spike, the server's system resources (memory, processor, bandwidth) are eaten up by the popular blog, taking resources away from your blog and slowing down service for your readers. Or perhaps a novice blogger attempts to install a piece of flawed code into his site and takes down the system. Casual bloggers can live with such risks, but if you want your site to be considered a reliable and professional service, the risk might not be worth it to you.

When you're shopping for a hosted blogging service, in addition to all the other concerns we've listed above, also take size and reputation of the service into account. Don't try to save a few bucks per month by going with a small and unknown service. Stick with names you can trust. Some quality services are recommended in Chapter 2.

The main advantages to hosted blogging services are that they are all easy to set up, have a relatively low cost of entry, and provide

Tip...

Smart Tip

Many blogging services offer free or low-cost plans. Try out a few before you select just one. Your time and money will be well spent.

decent features. If you're not known for being handy with server software installations, this may be the best choice for you.

Installed Server Applications

An installed server application is a program that you the user install on your own web server, or web host account. Available blogging server applications range in size and quality from small hobbyist scripts to large commercial applications. There are free, open-source applications and expensive, proprietary ones. Experiment with the open-source software blogging applications as it won't cost you anything to do so, and many of them are better quality than their commercial counterparts.

Running your own blogging application allows for infinite control over your blog. If you are familiar with the code in which the application was written, there's nothing stopping you from reaching into the code and making any changes you deem necessary. If you are not familiar with coding, you likely will find the application's base installation more than sufficient for your needs anyway. Don't let the idea of tinkering in code scare you away from this option; most users never find it necessary as most of these applications are well polished and easy-to-use. The details of downloading and installing some of these applications are covered in Chapter 2.

The main benefit of using an installed application is that you'll enjoy more control over every aspect of running your blog. The web server will be under your control (either humming along in your basement, or through your web hosting provider); the application will be under your control; the advertising integration will be under your control; and the system backups will be under your control. As you are the one depending on your blog for income, it makes sense that you would want the most control over the service you provide.

One major drawback to this method is that because you have all the control, you also have all of the responsibility. If the server goes down, it will be up to you to fix it (unless you are using a web hosting provider, who can help you with outages). If the blogging application won't load properly, it will be up to you to fix it. And if the advertising doesn't load properly, it will be up to you to make nice with your sponsors . . . and fix it.

You will need to register a domain name if you choose this method of running a blog, and you will likely need to pay hosting fees. This method may be more expensive for you in the beginning, but as your blog grows, your expenses will not grow with it as they will with a blogging service. That means that as your advertising or merchandising revenue rises, your profits won't be eaten up by higher service fees.

If you have no familiarity with hosting a web site, and this process seems daunting, do some research before choosing this path. It can be trying at times for those unfamiliar with web hosting, but it certainly can be learned, and is worth the time it takes to learn—especially if you plan on making your living running a web site.

Suitability for Your Content

When seeking a blogging platform be sure to consider your intended content. All the traffic analysis and ad network integration in the world won't help you if the service doesn't allow you to post photos on your photo blog. So the first thing to look for in a blogging service or application is the ability to handle the content you wish to include.

In most cases, a blog is simply text, links, and the occasional photo. So, in most cases, any blog service you choose will be able to handle all the content you need. But as the blogging phenomenon has expanded, so have the requirements of the bloggers. To keep up with the competition, you may need your blog to play sound clips, movies, cartoons, and more. Be sure to check out the feature lists of any blog platform you wish to use. If something is unclear, e-mail the programmers or service hosts.

Advertising Capacity

Many blogging services have built-in advertising capabilities. This often makes generating revenue at the beginning relatively easy. Popular ad networks such as BlogAds and Google's AdSense sometimes affiliate themselves with a particular blogging service to enable the users of that service to install their ads with the click of a mouse. This, obviously, has real benefits for the blogger when just starting out. It gets some money flowing with little effort. But once your blog begins drawing serious traffic and you outgrow that simple advertising strategy, it could cause problems for you. Integration of outside ad networks may not be allowed, or, if allowed, could be a technical pain to do.

Beware!
Some blogging services do not allow advertising by bloggers. Don't assume that your ads are allowed. Check first.

There will come a time in the life of your blog when you will need to solicit individual advertisers and belong to multiple ad networks. Therefore you should find a blogging service that not only makes advertising easy in the beginning, but also allows for expansion later on. Ask the blog service providers if they lock you into any one ad network, and if they allow access to your blog's template code for more ad integration later. Advertising integration is covered in more detail in Chapters 2 and 3.

Future Growth

Advertising isn't the only area where you should be concerned about growth. You should also consider growth in terms of blog traffic and storage space. If you choose to use a blog service, it may have traffic and storage maximums—especially for its free service. You may find out that as you grow, so will the fees you owe, which may or may not be a deciding factor for you.

Before signing up with any particular blogging service, carefully read its feature list. A blogging service's feature list will give you a good idea if you will be able to do what you would like to do with your blog. For example, if you know that you will need to post photographs, the blogging service's feature list will let you know if that's possible. At the most basic level, your blogging service will need to provide archiving, visitor comments, and easy-to-use posting tools. Also, archiving is a key feature to consider. You will need the ability to archive all your posts so that your readers can access anything you've written since you started the blog. Any professional blog should have an extensive archive—preferably searchable.

If you choose to host your own blogging software, archiving should be built into any application you choose, so that won't be as much of a problem. However, your web host will have similar traffic and storage restrictions as the blogging services. There are so many web hosts on the internet that finding a cheap and reliable host will not be difficult. Though be sure that if you do choose this route that the web host you choose provides the technologies that your selected blogging application requires.

Customization

As your blog grows and you become more familiar with the platform and subject you've chosen, you'll no doubt begin to fine tune the whole operation for better speed performance, search engine ratings, and so on. If you're using a hosted blogging service, the amount of tinkering you're allowed to do may be limited. Understandably, if the blogging service wants its service to remain fast and reliable, it cannot allow all of their customers access to its site's code for tinkering. Some sites do allow bloggers access to their blog templates, which allows for enough customization to satisfy the average blogger. If you're the type of person who likes to bury his hands in the

Dollar Stretcher

Using your own web host instead of a blogging service will allow you more room for growth per dollar spent.

> **Beware!**
> Customizing your blogging application code should only be undertaken by those who understand the programming language in which the application was written, and only if the application's user license allows. If you are looking to customize code, choose what's referred to as "open-source software."

guts of an engine to squeeze out the last little bit of horsepower, you may not be satisfied with customization restrictions. In your research of blogging services, ask about customization.

If you know already that you can't live with customization restrictions, your best bet is to use a blogging application on a separate web hosting account. There are plenty of blogging applications that allow bloggers to tinker to no end. Some make it easy with intricate configuration menus, and some require diving into the actual code itself. If you have no familiarity with the code in which the application was written, it is best to keep out of it. Learn the code somewhere else and then, when you're more comfortable with the system, take your shot. Risking your income and months or years of posts is not worth cutting your programming teeth.

Bringing on Staff or Contributors

The blogging business has lots of parts. There's the actual blogging, of course, but there are also the advertisers, the marketing, the accounting, the merchandising, and so on. Blogging is a fun business, but it is still a real business, and needs to be treated as such. No one person can run a reliable, successful, profitable business that serves the needs of thousands (or millions) of customers every day—which yours will hopefully do. As the business is getting started, your main goal should be to run a reliable blog while planning the business's structure for growth. You should not assume that you can do everything the business needs for as long as the business needs it. A blog must be updated every single day. Are you planning a life wherein you never get a vacation? Or even a weekend off?

In the beginning, you will likely do everything yourself. But there will come a point where you simply can't do everything you need to do in the course of the day. In addition to researching and writing posts for your blog, it is possible that you'll also be responsible for soliciting advertisers, managing advertising networks, processing merchandise orders, packing and shipping orders, e-mailing readers, and a thousand other little things. And that long list doesn't

> **Tip...**
>
> **Smart Tip**
> Plan to hire help. If you think of your blog as a business, not as a hobby, you will need to plan to have help.

even include all the responsibilities of your non-blogging personal life. As your business grows, taking care of all the peripheral work that building a successful blog requires, while posting frequently and reliably on the blog, will become impossible. Before you become overwhelmed by the amount of work required to keep your blog going, or definitely if you notice that the quality of your posts is beginning to suffer because you're too busy with the "back office" part of your blog business, it is time to hire help.

Unfortunately, many business owners need to reach a point of absolute frenzy before they realize they need to hire help. Essentially, in order to take on a full-time employee, the business owner often must overload himself with the work of two (or more) people just to build the business to the point that it can support another salary. Try not to wait for that point. Luckily, when just starting out, you likely will not need full-time help. A person or two, for a few hours a week, will significantly lighten your load and allow you to focus on delivering quality content to your readers.

Your Growth Plan

Before you even begin blogging you should have a plan for growth, as mentioned above. This plan should consist of your goals for your business (readership, revenue, profitability, etc.), a timeframe in which to achieve these goals, and a map of the employees you will need to get there.

Business Goals

The goals for a blogging business are unique to every blogger. Some prefer to blog in their spare time for extra cash, some have a career in mind, some aim for world domination. When deciding your goals, take into account the level of intricacy you're prepared to deal with and the amount of time you want to spend. A small blog with one advertising network is obviously less complicated and time consuming than a huge blog with private sponsors, three ad networks, and coffee mugs for sale. Make a short list of three or four goals for your blog, and write them at the top of your growth plan.

Your Timeframe

Construct a reasonable and conservative timeframe in which you expect to achieve these goals. If you have planned a modest blog, aim for achieving your desired readership levels in nine months to a year. If you have considerably more ambitious goals, achieving your desired level of readership could take anywhere from two to four years. Some blogs have caught on much faster, but you should not count on that level of success. It will take considerable time for your readership to grow, come to trust you, and refer their like-minded friends. If you haven't reached your goal within four years, or have stopped growing for several months at any point along the way, you should re-evaluate your marketing strategies.

Your Employee Map

Perhaps the most valuable employee-related planning you can do now, to save you worry and stress down the road, is to create an employee map. This map is a plan for future positions and future employees. Devise a map that plots out all the possible positions you can think of, include brief job descriptions, and where the positions fall in your business and on your timeline.

First plan out the employees that you will need immediately. What do you envision taking up most of your time as your blog grows? If you are selling merchandise, consider part-time shipping help to give you more time to write for your blog. If you are selling advertising space to private sponsors, consider a part-time marketer to attract more advertisers to your page. Once you get help with the most time-consuming area of your start-up business, you'll have some free time to devote to the other areas of your business that require your attention.

Next, plan out the secondary positions you would like to fill. These might be the services that would be better left to a professional, such as bookkeeping or writing advertising agreements. Or, hire someone to promote your blog to expedite growth. With these jobs out of the way, you should be able to devote your time to doing what you do best—providing quality content for your blog audience.

Your Employee Map will be a useful tool both in terms of helping you make quicker decisions when the time comes to begin hiring, and giving you a clear view of where your business should be headed. Refer to this map as a guideline for the direction for growth of the business.

Hiring Contributors

You may begin to feel swamped by the responsibility of writing several blog posts per day. If you think that your time would be better

Beware!
Stepping back from posting entirely could backfire. Be sure to watch the posted material closely and act as an editor when necessary.

spent working on other aspects of the business, you could hire or enlist the help of volunteer blog contributors. The best place to find such help is among your readership. The people who visit your blog regularly have already displayed a sincere interest in your content. There are a few among them who would love a chance to begin writing for their favorite blog. There's a thrill in being a reader-turned-poster; most readers would jump at the chance to post to the blog without pay. This may seem like a wonderful situation, and it may well be, but you should be careful when accepting volunteer help.

First, you would have a hard time imposing quotas on volunteer help. Asking for daily content from volunteers would be asking a lot. And, if you decide that the volunteer you've enlisted is not producing the quality of post that you would like, you'll have a harder time asking her to stop. Paying contributors, even a small stipend, makes it easier to set a minimum number of posts per day and to "fire" posters that don't produce quality.

You should plan to serve as editor for any posters you hire, at least for a period of time to evaluate the quality of content that he or she will produce for you. You cannot take the risk of hiring help without editorial rights. Your blog could suffer heavily from an incompetent, unreliable, or uninformed blogger. Until you can trust that a certain person will reliably produce worthy content for you, insist that everything he or she posts passes through you first. This will create more work for you in the short term, as you'll be writing your own posts while editing others, but it will pay off in the long run if you can find reliable help.

If you are able to find several reliable contributors—enough to cover your daily posting duties—you could conceivably get out of posting to your blog altogether and focus on finding more readers, advertisers, and therefore, profits. That is, if that's the part of the blogging business you like best.

Planning Wrap-Up

Take as long as you need to effectively plan your blog. There is no better time to tinker and test your business idea that before you get started. After launch you will have committed your time and money to one path or another, so try to be sure when heading into the venture that it is the right one.

Review your plans once they are complete and make sure that you have built a solid plan for growth. If you know someone with blog experience, consider having her or

▲

him review your plan. You should feel as though you have considered every aspect of the business as possible—that you've exhausted all the possibilities. You should also *be* exhausted, and you have every right to be. Planning a profitable business, especially one in a new industry like blogging, requires a lot of time and brainpower. But if you've done your job well, you will have built a solid foundation from which your blog and business will grow.

Print your plan. Take a nap. Have a nourishing meal. Then come back to this book for Chapter 2 where you'll tackle the most exciting part of your new business: setting up your blog.

Publishing Your Blog

You have an almost inexhaustible number of blog services and blog applications to test and tinker with before deciding upon one. The process can be overwhelming. The most promising of the blogging services and applications are collected here in this chapter to give you a good headstart on finding a blog platform that works for you.

There are many books, web sites, and even blogs devoted to helping first-time users get set up with each of the services and applications discussed below. Also, each service covered here provides extensive instructions for either registering for, or installing, the service. Detailing each process step-by-step here would be redundant, quickly out of date, and beyond the scope of this book's intended purpose. Instead, this chapter will go over the virtues and failings of each service to help you make a more informed decision. Consult each individual service's web site at the URLs provided for the latest feature information and the best instructions on how to begin using their services or applications.

Community Blogging Services

As blogging grows in popularity, many web sites that did not offer blogging services originally have begun to do so. For example, many community web sites such as Friendster, MySpace, and Facebook all now offer blogs to each of their members. These community blog services are basic and are usually used only as online gossip journals for teenagers and 'tweens. They do not allow outside advertising; therefore, unless you are planning your blog revenue to be based solely on non-advertising sources, such as merchandising, these services are not for you.

These services also tend to be provincial—internet-wise. While these communities do offer external links to user blogs so that nonmembers of the community can read them, they tend to be unsuccessful at drawing in readers from outside the member community. This is due to the nature of their content, the specialized intentions of the bloggers, and the aversion audiences have to nonpublic blogging. For example, a blog published on a community service (www.examplecommunity.com) will have a community service address (www.examplecommunity.com/username). People will assume, often correctly, that a visitor will need to register as a member of that community in order to access the blog. The aversion to registering with communities just to read a blog will turn readers away.

 Beware! Portal and community blog sites do not target their blog services at professional bloggers and therefore are lacking the features on which professionals depend.

The large portal sites have also gotten in on the blogging game recently with the introduction of services like MSN's Spaces and Yahoo!'s 360. These services are also rather remedial at this point, but do offer the posting of photos and template personalization. Yahoo!'s 360 service offers integration with LAUNCHcast, their Yahoo!Music radio station service. And MSN's Spaces actually offers room on their blogs for users to insert their own advertising through Amazon Associates or Kanoodle, a contextual textual advertising network.

Even though MSN's Spaces allows you to earn an income from their blog service, the ads from which you earn a revenue would be competing with the ads that make money for MSN. You must share your page with MSN's advertisers, and therefore your click-through rate plummets.

All of the blogging services from MySpace, Friendster, Facebook, MSN, and Yahoo! are targeted toward the casual blogger who uses a blog to keep in touch with family and friends. For your purposes, you should use a more robust, flexible service or application like the ones featured below.

Web-Based Blogging Services

Each of the services below are hosted blogging services as described in this chapter. These are some of the most popular services, but they are by no means the only quality services available. Research each of them and seek out some others in your spare time. You'll be surprised to see how much hosted blogging services vary in features and price and flexibility.

Blogger

Blogger was launched in 1999 by Pyra Labs, a software company in San Francisco and was one of the pioneers of the blogging movement. Some credit Blogger for popularizing the blog format, and even the term "blog." In 2003, the service was purchased and made free to the public by Google, the Mountain View, California, search engine juggernaut. Google continued the development of Blogger and in 2004 it integrated their Picasa and Hello services to allow for easy posting of photos. Soon after, Google unveiled a new version of Blogger that boasted new, powerful features such as CSS-compliant templates, better archiving of posts, and posting via e-mail. (A new version of Blogger with more features is scheduled for release by Spring 2007.)

Blogger is the most commonly used blogging service on the internet. First-time bloggers enjoy that Blogger is fast to set up, easy to use, and does not charge a cent for any of its services. No programming skills are necessary to set up a blog on the service, all the tools are point-and-click. Blogger also does not limit users in terms of traffic, storage space, or even the number of blogs you can create.

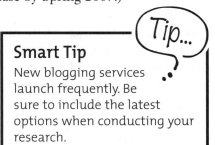

Smart Tip

New blogging services launch frequently. Be sure to include the latest options when conducting your research.

Blogger offers many advanced features. It allows for visitor comments, which you moderate; visitor comments can be integral in building a community around your blog. It makes photo uploads easy, and even allows photo posting from a mobile camera phone with their Blogger Mobile service. Blogger will also, if you choose, automatically alert weblogs.com, the popular list of recently updated blogs, every time you update your blog. But most importantly, it automatically integrates with Google's AdSense service, allowing you to begin earning revenue instantly by selecting a few options in your account's settings. Blogger is by far the fastest "idea-to-income" blogging service available.

Blogger also allows you access to the code of your blog templates, which means that you have the ability to display advertisements from private sponsors and other non-Google ad networks.

Once you have registered for an account—and we suggest you do, if only to test it out—you will be asked to specify your "Blog*Spot" address. The "Blog*Spot" is where the Blogger blogs are published. Blogger is the blog creation tool, and Blog*Spot is where they're hosted on the web. This can be a rather confusing setup, but Blogger makes the whole process seamless. Your Blog*Spot address is a fancy term for your blog's URL, and will have the following format: http://yourblog.blogspot.com. You are free to change the "yourblog" portion of that address to anything you wish as long as it is not already taken, vulgar, or contains URL-unfriendly characters.

As a professional blogger, hosting your blog as a subdomain of blogspot.com (or any host) is not acceptable. You will need to register your own domain name and set it, within your chosen registrar's domain name manager, to redirect all traffic to your Blog*Spot address. If you'd like even more control over your blog, Blogger makes more advanced methods of publishing available.

In addition to using the default setting of publishing your blog on Blog*Spot, Blogger allows bloggers to publish blogs on third-party web hosts. This is not a download version of the Blogger blog tool. Rather, it is a method of publishing where bloggers use the Blogger web site to create their blogs, just as they normally would, but upon clicking "Publish" their blog is sent to their specified server instead of to Blog*Spot. This option is easy to set up, and provides the added advantages of more web server control and the freedom from Blogger's occasional service outages. You will need to register your own domain name and find a web host before you can begin using this method.

You will run your blogs from your Dashboard—the main control panel for your administration section. All your Blogger blogs are listed on your main Dashboard site, with links to their individual management and posting pages. From your Dashboard,

you can configure, post to, or delete any blog in your account. Clicking on an individual blog name presents you with the options of creating or editing posts, moderating visitor comments, viewing status, changing settings, changing the site's aesthetic template, adding AdSense, and more. Once you've created your first blog, click through the different options and features available to you.

If you're interested in giving Blogger a try, go to www.blogger.com and click "Create Your Blog Now." The site will walk you through the simple process.

TypePad

TypePad was launched in 2003 by Six Apart Ltd., another San Franciscan software company, as an online blogging service. The base program, Movable Type (which is covered later in this chapter) was written by Ben Trott to allow his wife (cofounder of Six Apart Ltd.), Mena, to easily produce her own blog. The new blogging application was made available for download and enjoyed immediate success. This success led to the development of the web-based version of the platform, in the form of TypePad. In 2004, Six Apart Ltd. was able to purchase Danga Interactive, the parent company of rival blogging service LiveJournal, which was quickly integrated into Six Apart Ltd.'s offerings. The new, merged, company now has over seven million users.

TypePad has become a popular service even though, unlike Blogger, it is not free. It offers different levels of service with prices ranging from $4.95 to $14.95 per month. Professional bloggers prefer TypePad to Blogger because it does not cater to the beginner crowd. The service focuses on powerful features, attractive and easy-to-navigate blogs, extensive customization, and easy integration of revenue streams.

TypePad provides highly customizable sidebars, which is a benefit to any professional blogger. These sidebars, through modules that TypePad calls TypeLists, can be configured to hold advertisements, photo albums, Amazon.com book links, music, and anything else you can insert by pasting a snippet of code. This means that you're not stuck with one advertising network, blogroll template, or revenue stream. You have complete control of your sidebar content.

TypePad also provides automatic notification of www.weblogs.com and www.blogs.com, the two most popular services displaying recently updated blogs. TypePad provides archiving of posts, the depth of which depends on your service subscription. It allows for the integration of podcasting and video support, scheduling posts, posting via e-mail or mobile device, publishing of RSS feeds, and some of the most attractive default templates available. As you can see, TypePad goes out of its way to be the most fully-featured web-based blogging service available.

In addition to allowing for outside advertising networks, TypePad offers some revenue-producing services of their own to Pro users: TipJar and TypePad Text Ads. The setup of these services is comparable to the easy setup of Blogger's Google AdSense ads. You simple designate that you would like to take advantage of these features in your blog settings, and you're all set to begin earning money. TypePad also provides a tool to track your earnings over time.

TipJar is a simple donation feature that allows your blog readers to contribute financially to your blog. All donations are deposited into your TypePad earning account, which can then be credited against your TypePad subscription fees or deposited into a PayPal account. Some restrictions apply, however; for example, you must have a balance of at least $15.01 before you can transfer money out of your TypePad account. All amounts below $15.00 are credited to your site service fees.

TypePad's Text Ads are textual ads that will appear in the sidebar of your site, wherever you choose. These ads are automatically provided by TypePad and change depending on the subject of the page on which they happen to be displayed. They function and appear almost identically to Google's AdSense ads. You are paid for each valid click on any of the ads displayed. The money earned per click depends on the ad that is being displayed; you will have no way of knowing which ads pay what amount. All the money earned is deposited into your TypePad account and can be either credited toward your TypePad fees or deposited to a PayPal account. The same amount restrictions apply to your TypePad earnings that apply to your TipJar earnings.

Both of these services are handy and are easily integrated into your TypePad blog. But it should be pointed out that in order to take advantage of these two services, you must subscribe to their Pro level of service which, at this writing, is $14.95 per month. While upgrading

Beware!
Blogging services that provide their own advertising delivery systems may not allow bloggers to use outside ad networks. Check to be sure before signing on to a service. It may not matter to you at the beginning, but you'll want to know what your limitations are.

your account to this level improves the service you receive in myriad ways (more storage, more blogs, more archives, etc.), it should not be done solely to take advantage of these two services.

If you are looking to accept donations, which is covered more extensively in Chapter 3, you can bypass TypePad's more expensive monthly service and set up an account with PayPal directly. PayPal will charge you per transaction, but there is no monthly fee, and the setup on your blog is quite simple. Likewise, if you're looking to set up text ads on your site, you can sign up with Google's AdSense and set them up directly on your blog as well. You can have more flexible equivalents to the TipJar and Text Ads service for a fraction more work and far less expense per month.

TypePad is a good service and any professional blogger would do well to select it. There are ways to give your blog a more professional appearance, such as selection of your own domain name, customization of your template, and integration of third-party ad networks, but even at its default set up, TypePad produces a respectable blog. Visit their web site at www.typepad.com.

WordPress.com

WordPress.com is a free blogging service, like Blogger, that is tailored to casual bloggers needing easy-to-use features. It is the web-based offspring of the downloadable WordPress blogging application, available at www.wordpress.org (covered later in this chapter). WordPress got its start as b2\cafelog, another blogging application, but was spun-off into the more robust WordPress application. The success of the WordPress application spawned the web-based WordPress.com hosted blogging service.

WordPress.com functions much like Blogger. Users control their blogs through a Dashboard that lets them write and edit posts, manage sidebars, templates, and whatnot. All the available features are easy to implement and configure. The difference between WordPress.com and Blogger is most clear when it comes to available customization. The current version of Blogger does not offer much in the way of customization to begin with, but WordPress.com manages to offer even less. Where Blogger stresses options, Word Press.com stresses restrictions.

You are limited to publishing one blog through your WordPress.com account. Of course you could sign up for individual accounts ad infinitum, but you would need to log in to each account separately to manage each individual blog. WordPress.com allows you to manage the information in the vertical sidebars running along the sides of your blog

Dollar Stretcher

Even free blogging services vary greatly in quality and features available. Don't assume that all the free services offer the same basic service. Some are quite well-equipped.

but does not give you access to any code, making real customization impossible. Also, you're stuck with the templates they provide.

The real deal-breaker is that WordPress.com makes it clear that advertising networks, or commercial blogging of any kind, is frowned upon. From their Frequently Asked Questions page:

"We have a very low tolerance for blogs created purely for search engine optimization or commercial purposes, machine-generated blogs, and will continue to nuke them, so if that's what you're interested in [WordPress.com] is not for you."

While they make a good point that there are some forms of commercially motivated blogs that are machine-generated and used solely for profiting purposes, it also makes clear that they do not want their service to become a hotbed of blogging businesses.

In the same article on their Frequently Asked Questions page, they concede that while they currently do not permit AdSense or any other advertising network to be used on their service, they may relent on this issue in the future.

So, at least for the present time, signing up with WordPress.com with commercial blogging intentions would be a bad idea. With no advertising capabilities, limited control over your sidebars, and little template customization, you'd have a hard time turning a profit. To check out WordPress.com for yourself, visit www.wordpress.com.

Eponym

At the time of this book's printing, Eponym is only a few months old, and virtually unknown around the blogosphere. It is a small, ten-employee company, based in Fayetteville, Arkansas, and currently hosts under 10,000 blogs. On the first day of their unadvertised launch, they signed up only ten bloggers. But in the two months that followed, word began to spread quickly, and they are currently receiving 400 new blogger registrations a day. They are very much aware of professional bloggers, and their service reflects it. Eponym is a great service and is one to keep an eye on.

If TypePad is trying to be the most feature-rich web-based blogging service, the folks over at Eponym are giving them a run for their money. Across their six levels of service, ranging in price from free to $39.95 per month, they offer just about everything a professional blogger could want.

Their free service rivals the pay services of many other web-based blogging services. This may be due to the fact that blogs using their free service display compulsory textual ads that earn revenue for Eponym itself. You still have the ability to add ads of your own, but they will be competing with Eponym's ads, which can only hurt your revenue.

Upon subscribing to any of the pay service levels, the compulsory ads are removed from your blog, along with all other Eponym branding. This is quite an offer, as most blogging services, even pay services, will leave their logo somewhere on your blog for branding purposes.

Upgrading to a pay service also provides you with more traffic capability, more storage space, and personal e-mail support. Also, as a tip of the hat to professional bloggers, Eponym offers a "Custom Web Address" feature. The default Eponym address takes the same form that all the other services provide: http://your blog.eponym.com. The Custom Web Address feature allows you to add two more addresses, in addition to your default Eponym address. These addresses could be either two more Eponym subdomains, such as http://tutti.eponym.com and http://frutti.eponym.com, or they could be two top-level domains, such as www.mytuttiblog.com and www.myfruttiblog.com, or they could be one of each.

The fact that Eponym is offering the ability to use top-level domains for blogs on their service is somewhat misleading. It a worthwhile service, but what exactly it is they're offering can be confusing. They are not offering domain name registration, and they try to make that clear. They are not offering to configure your domain name to point to your blog. And, any person with a registered domain name and some know-how can point that domain name to any web address they wish. So what are they offering? What the Custom Web Address feature does for top-level domain holders is configure Eponym's own server to recognize visitors to the domain, and internally redirect it to the user's blog. This is not the same as a simple redirect where the web address that the visitor sees changes once they have been redirected. This service allows blog owners to use their own domain names on Eponym's servers, making Eponym totally invisible to visitors. Misleading though it is at first, this is a valuable service and makes life much easier for professional bloggers.

All the feature upgrades listed above are available with any pay services they offer. The cheapest plan is $4.95 per month. From there the next four levels of service are stratified by amount of storage space and traffic capacity offered.

Dollar Stretcher

Eponym's Custom Web Address feature allows bloggers to have their own ".com" without paying monthly fees for a web hosting server.

The functionality of the service itself is similar to the other web-based services. You control your unlimited number of blogs through . . . you guessed it . . . the Dashboard. What makes Eponym stand out from the crowd is the level of customization it makes available. Not only does it have a gallery of useful widgets to add to your blog's sidebars, but it allows you to create your own using your own HTML and JavaScript code. This means you can display any ad network you want, as well as donation buttons, custom blogrolls, and invite private sponsors. You have full control.

Not only does Eponym offer all the features you would expect such as archiving, RSS feeds, posting via e-mail and mobile device, and a word-processor-like editing tool, but it also offers features you wouldn't expect, such as built-in image editing, slideshows, posting categories, and much more. To see a complete list of features and how Eponym compares to other web-based blogging services, go to www.eponym.com/compare.php.

Not only is Eponym highly customizable and easy to use, it seems to be managed with professional bloggers in mind. If you are looking for a web-based platform from which to run your blog, we recommend giving Eponym a whirl. Be sure to upgrade to one of its pay services for the full experience. For $4.95, it's worth it. Visit Eponym at www.eponym.com.

Installed Server Applications

As mentioned earlier, an Installed Server Application is a blogging program that you must download and install on a web server. Each of the following applications comes with extensive instructions on how to install the application on a web server, and what is necessary to do so. This can be a tricky process, as there are many factors involved. This book is not intended to be an FTP, Unix, PHP/MySQL, Perl manual. There are plenty of great books available if you would like to learn about the technical aspects of this process. As with web-based services, the focus here is on reviewing each application for its worthiness as a platform for your blogging business. If you find yourself intimidated by the idea of installing your own application, you might want to consider one of the web-based services. However, if you know how to wrestle an application onto a server, or if you're up for learning the task, an Installed Server Application can provide bloggers with more control, and more ability to customize, than a hosted blogging service ever could.

Below are some of the most widely used and reliably supported blogging applications.

Movable Type

Movable Type is a proprietary blogging application developed by Six Apart Ltd., the company that also offers TypePad, profiled above. Movable Type is a widely-used blogging platform with many of the features you would expect such as archiving, trackback, and visitor comments. It is also extensible, which means that the large user community has the ability to develop and install plug-ins to enhance the application's usefulness. It is free to individual users, but must be licensed to enable its multiple contributor and multiple blog capabilities.

Movable Type has many advantages for the professional blogger. First, it has been in use and development since 2001. This means that there are many experienced users of Movable Type who have published web sites, books, reviews, and articles to help you become familiar with the platform. If you find yourself lost while installing, configuring, or using Movable Type, a search on Google or Amazon will quickly lead you to a solution. The Learning Movable Type web site (www.learningmovabletype.com) is also a great place to start.

Due to the fact that Movable Type is so widely used, Six Apart Ltd. has been able to enlist the help of a few web hosts around the internet who will either install Movable Type for you on your hosting account, or will have it already installed when you sign up. This service can greatly ease your installation, but limits you to the six or seven hosting companies that offer it. For a complete list of Movable Type's hosting partners, visit www.sixapart.com/movabletype/hosting.

Another advantage is the application's networking capabilities, which can come in handy when trying to spread the word about your new business venture. Movable Type introduced the concept of TrackBack to the blogosphere with their release of version 2.2 in 2002. TrackBack can be hard to understand fully; Wikipedia does the best job of explaining it. Here's their description:

Dollar Stretcher

Finding a web host that bundles a blogging application into its service is not hard to do and could save you some money.

"TrackBack is a mechanism for the communication between blogs: if a blogger writes a new entry commenting on, or referring to, an entry found at another blog, and both blogging tools support the TrackBack protocol, then the commenting blogger can notify the other blog with a "TrackBack ping"; the receiving blog will typically display summaries of, and links to, all the commenting entries below the original entry. This allows for conversations spanning several blogs that readers can easily follow." (Reprinted from http://en.wikipedia.org/wiki/TrackBack under the GNU Free Documentation License, available at www.gnu.org/copy left/fdl.html)

Apart from its technologically confusing nature, TrackBack is a great way to get a lot of links to your blog scattered around the blogosphere in a hurry. And it can bring in hordes of readers at a time.

The interface of Movable Type is similar to TypePad's. It will list all your blogs for you on your main page (or just your one, if you haven't purchased a license). Clicking on your blog title will bring you to your blog management page where you can perform all the tasks that you would expect, like posting and editing entries, managing categories, templates, and so on.

The text formatting capabilities offered when posting to your blog are pretty basic. You might see this as an advantage or disadvantage. On the one hand, most times you don't need all the fancy WYSIWYG (What You See Is What You Get) capabilities of a word-processor-like text box, and it just slows page loading. On the other hand, being able to bold, underline, and insert links without learning HTML or Movable Type's shorthand codes could be useful.

A larger disadvantage is that Movable Type's feature set is pretty basic overall. It is, no question, a solid blogging application, but for users who are accustomed to state-of-the-art web-based formatting, image, and customization tools like on Eponym and the upcoming version of Blogger, Movable Type comes up short.

In fact, the basic installation of Movable Type does not even allow swapping of blog templates—a feature that should be standard with every blog service. Movable Type does allow bloggers access to their template code, which means that customizing your blog's appearance requires intimate familiarity with CSS and HTML. A feature as seemingly simple as inserting a list of links in one of your blog's sidebars requires opening the code for the blog template, searching for the specific code that creates the sidebar, and editing it to taste. This process seems extraordinarily labored when compared to something like Eponym's drag-and-drop sidebar manager.

Dollar Stretcher

TrackBack, a method of communicating between blogs, can be an effective form of free advertising.

Dollar Stretcher

Time is money. The more time you spend fiddling with your blog's coding, the less time you'll have to produce money-making content. Find useful plug-ins to speed up common tasks.

Imagine the task of entirely rewriting the CSS and HTML template code to give your blog a unique aesthetic look. It is the only option for users of the basic installation, and it is unnecessarily daunting. But luckily the talented devotees of Movable Type agree, and have produced an essential plug-in that, once installed, allows for the quick swapping in and out of blog templates. There are many such helpful plug-ins available to cut down on the grueling nature of some of Movable Type's tasks. To see all of the plug-ins available for Movable Type, visit www.sixapart.com/pronet/plugins/.

While there is an extensive library of free-to-use plug-ins to search, unfortunately there is not a magical plug-in to streamline every rough edge in Movable Type. Integrating any ad network, other than Chitika eMiniMalls, for which, Movable Type provides a plug-in, still requires involved coding.

One of Movable Type's failings is that it relies so heavily on contributed plug-ins to extend its usefulness, but that is one of its virtues as well. Movable Type enthusiasts are contributing to the plug-in library every day, and with every contribution Movable Type gets even better. This is a distinct advantage over other blogging applications that rely solely on a few employed developers to program everything.

Overall, Movable Type can be a powerful blogging platform. The learning curve to achieve its maximum potential is steep, but ultimately can take you quite high. If you want to use an already-powerful platform that is far easier to use, and functions similarly to Movable Type, try TypePad. But, if you feel ready to invest yourself in a platform and dedicate the next few months to exploring plug-ins, becoming familiar with bits of code, and researching help, then Movable Type will prove to be a powerful platform for you. Movable Type is available at www.sixapart.com/movabletype.

LifeType

LifeType is an open-source blogging platform that has been, since its launch in 2003 designed from the ground up to allow multiple blogs with multiple contributors in the hope of creating many strong blog communities. It began as pLog, a multi-user, multi-blog platform that was extensible, and supported different design templates and language localization. The legend goes that Amazon.com, which for some reason owns the trademark for "plog," asked the pLog folks to change the name of their project. LifeType was born.

LifeType is still, in many respects, a young blogging platform but that does not mean it fails to pull its own weight. It has some decent advantages right off the bat.

First, it's free. Being an open-source project, it is free to download, use, redistribute, and even alter if you wish. You will never run into licensing issues with LifeType, no matter what your intended use, number of installs, or number of contributors. Second, it boasts a "smarter than the average bear" installation wizard which simplifies the often brutal task of installing a

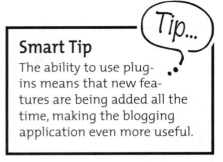

Smart Tip
The ability to use plug-ins means that new features are being added all the time, making the blogging application even more useful.

complex database-driven application to a web server. And third, like Movable Type, it is extensible. This means that the user community surrounding the project has the ability to develop and donate plug-ins to make LifeType more powerful.

In addition to these early advantages, and all the usual blogging platform features, LifeType also provides some unexpected bonuses. Search-engine-friendly URLs is one example. Most blogging platforms construct URLs for your posts that look like this:

http://yourblog.blogservice.com/index.php?articleId=2&parentId=179&blogId=1

This address tells the search engine bots, which are constantly crawling around the internet searching for keywords, nothing about the contents of the post to which it links.

LifeType, if you ask it to, will format your post's URLs to provide useful information to both the reader and to the search engine bots. These friendlier URLs look like this:

http://yourblog.blogservice.com/yourBlogName/archive/
527_A_Post_Description.html

As you can see, it is much easier to read by humans—and keyword-hunting machines. A few other blogging platforms can perform this function for you, including Movable Type and WordPress.

Another neat feature is that LifeType is localizable. This means that the whole blog can be easily set up to run in another language. So, if you have an international audience, and can blog in German, Spanish, Dutch, French, and so on, TypePad will work well for you.

Beware!
Localization means that the labels on your blog applications functions and features will be translated for readers of other languages, not your content.

LifeType also supports podcasting, mass file uploads, photo albums, blogging from a mobile device, and many other fun features.

The downside of LifeType is that its administrative interface can be confusing. The menus and options are not intuitive, and you might find yourself searching for the tools you need. Also, there is no easy way to integrate an ad network into your blog. You will need to find and search through your template code for the correct section to edit.

LifeType has many admirable qualities, but falls short when it comes to delivering a blogging platform suited to professional blogging. If you're looking for a more user-friendly, more easily customizable platform, try Blogger or Eponym. But like with Movable Type, if you are comfortable reading and editing code, LifeType likely won't pose any problems for you. For more information, visit www.lifetype.com.

b2evolution

Like WordPress, b2evolution also forked off the abandoned b2\cafelog project. b2evolution is a multi-contributor, multi-blog, open-source platform that supports language localization. It is free and, like LifeType, comes with an installation wizard for easy setup.

Like the other applications we've profiled, a main page displays the user's blogs and configuration tabs. Clicking through the tabs allows the user to tinker with the usual configurations: categories, posts, template files. The sheer number of available tabs and subtabs in b2evolution speak to the applications many features, but can be a bit overwhelming at first. It will take any user a considerable amount of time before feeling at home among the maze of tabs.

b2evolution is not set up with professional bloggers in mind. Placing custom content in sidebars involves editing template files; there is no easy way to integrate with an ad network; and customizing the look of your site requires knowledge of CSS and HTML.

Like a few of the other applications, this latest version of b2evolution is extensible, so there are plug-ins available to make some tasks easier, and more are being developed every day.

b2evloution is a young application (they haven't even released version 1.0) and therefore, take this profile with that in mind. Version 1.6 is in beta at the time of this printing, and promises to deliver some genuine improvements in the overall appearance and functionality of the application.

There are a few places where b2evolution stands out. The traffic statistics that the application collects and displays are some of the best internal stats seen to date, both in terms of amount of data collected and how that data is displayed. The traffic summary is displayed in a

> **Tip...**
>
> **Smart Tip**
> Watching your blog's traffing closely will provide you with a good idea of your audience's reading habits, interests, and locations. You'll learn who is coming to see what, from where, and at what time. All useful stuff.

▲

Beware!

Comment SPAM is a real problem and can make your blog an unattractive destination for your readers.

Flash-animated chart that is far more attractive and easy to read than the raw server log files. Version 1.6 promises to improve upon an already impressive statistic tracking tool.

b2evolution also has robust anti-spam filters that you can customize to suit your needs. Comment spam is becoming a large problem across the blogosphere as spammers grow more clever. Spambots are able to roam freely across the blogs posting advertisements for nefarious sundries on every blog they pass. b2evolution allows you to automatically seek out and delete these advertisements as they are posted. It is the first blogging platform to so rigorously address this problem.

While the young b2evolution isn't quite up to snuff when compared to older, highly-polished applications, it shows promise. b2evolution is available at www.b2 evolution.net.

WordPress

While speaking of highly-polished blogging applications, WordPress deserves a mention. This application is the precursor to the WordPress.com web-based service. It is a free, open-source application, which means that you have access to all the code, and can customize the whole application top to bottom. It also means that WordPress, the company, doesn't have to (or get to) saddle the application with the protective restrictions they place on their hosted WordPress.com service.

We're happy to say that where the WordPress.com service fails, the WordPress application excels. The WordPress platform thrives in an unrestricted environment. Not only have the developers chosen to allow access to the template code, making customization possible, but they have gone one step further than all the other applications and called out the code in the places that most often receive customization. This makes customizing your blog's sidebars, headers, footers, comments, archives, posts, and everything else easier than in every other installed blogging application we profiled. You will still need to brave dealing directly with template code in places, but WordPress makes it significantly less daunting by pointing out what code to edit.

WordPress also allows you to not only create posts for you blog, but to create pages for your site. Their Pages manager makes it easy to create static informational pages on any topic you choose. This makes it simple to create an About Me page, a Contact Me page, a Merchandise Page, or even a good-natured

Tip...

Smart Tip

Adding entire new pages filled with custom content to your blog can make growth much easier, It also allows bloggers to provide nonpost content.

> ## Smart Tip
>
> Tip...
>
> As you'll be spending much of your work day using your blogging application's user interface, it is important that you pick one that you find attractive and easy to use.

Blogtastic! page. This is an extremely useful feature and has been largely ignored by other applications.

WordPress, like Movable Type and LifeType, is extensible and, at the time of this printing, is in the process of building a huge plug-in directory. For the time being, they have linked to four sites dedicated to WordPress plug-ins, each with a sizable number to offer. In total, we see well over 1,000 plug-ins available to make WordPress even more powerful.

There are several plug-ins available that make integrating Google's AdSense into WordPress quick and painless. There are also plug-ins to help you integrate eMiniMalls, Amazon.com, and others revenue streams. This seems to be the only installed application that allows bloggers to integrate with several ad networks without touching a single line of code.

WordPress offers a good number of aesthetic themes that you can install for your blog, and links to four web sites that offer even more. You won't have a hard time finding a theme to fit your needs, and if you can't find that perfect theme you had in mind, you have the ability to edit the code until you get exactly what you want.

The WordPress administrative interface works on the Dashboard concept, just like the WordPress.com service. The interface is attractive and easy to navigate. Tools do not get lost in an endless sea of tabs. You should quickly feel at home clicking through the numerous configuration options.

In addition to all these advantages, WordPress offers all the standard features that you've come to expect from a blogging service, and because it is run from your own server or web host, you won't run into service limits and price increases. It is a high-powered blogging platform with great extensibility and an easy-to-use nature. Oh, and it's free. We recommend it highly. And, conveniently, if you find that you would like to switch from your current blogging platform to WordPress, the application's Import tool can help you migrate from many of the top blogging services such as Blogger, LiveJournal, and Movable Type.

One of the few places where WordPress seems to be lacking is in the installation process. While installation instructions are plainly available on the WordPress web site, the process is still daunting for first-timers. An installation assistant that walks users through each step would complete this application nicely. Visit WordPress at www.wordpress.org.

• • •

Well, there you have it—eight of the most popular blogging platforms summed up in one convenient chapter. Keep in mind that these are active projects and are therefore continually developing new services. They have all likely made improvements since the publication of this book. So it would be worth it for you to visit their web sites, at the links provided, and read up on what's been recently added or fixed or changed. Then be sure to carefully consider whether you would like the ease of use of a web-based blogging service or the powerful customization of an application installed on a separate web server. Try a few possibilities before you commit to just one.

Once you have chosen and registered for, or installed, a platform for your blogging business, it is time to take another break. You now have your blogging business plan, the publishing platform on which to build that business, and now all you need . . . is some business! So rest up, because when you come back you'll begin Chapter 3—devoted to the most exciting (and exhausting) part of the three "P" process: Profiting!

3

Profiting from Your Blog

Everybody wants to get paid to do what they love. Blogging is a great way to earn some money while working with the topics you're passionate about. It isn't always easy, and the best way to do it isn't always clear. But you chose a topic that you're passionate about, the hard work you will need to put in while building your blogging business just won't

▲

seem like work. It's a fun day when you can spend eight to ten hours playing with your favorite hobby, and then come home with a paycheck.

As we mentioned in the beginning of Chapter 1, you will need to attain just three things to have a profitable blog. They are:

1. a steady stream of content
2. a large audience
3. a reliable revenue source

By now, you know how to maintain a steady stream of content and the best way to plan your blog to attract a large audience. What you still need to be clear about is how to let that large audience know where to find your blog and how to profit when it does. Chapter 3 discusses advertising for your blog, advertisers on your blog, other revenue streams, and the various ways to attain each.

How to Begin the Blog

So, now that you've got your plan ready and your publishing system is all set up, it is finally time to begin blogging. Before you can go out and find legions of faithful readers, you need something for them to actually read. Building a blog from the ground up takes some time, and may be frustratingly slow for some, but there's no way around it—you must have posts before you have profits.

The First Post

It may seem like a throw-away post, because you have no readers when you write it and you may think no one will ever read it except for you and the GoogleBot, but your blog's first post is one of its most important. Not only does it mark the beginning of your blogging career, but it announces to the blogosphere that there's a new voice in town. Archived first posts receive a considerable amount of traffic on popular blogs. Readers are often curious to learn how this blog that has become a part of their daily lives got its start, and so they seek out the first post.

The first post sets the tone of the blog, not only for your readers, but for yourself. You need to find your "blogger voice," and the quest begins here. This is not a matter of content. This concerns style. What impression would you like to give readers? Do you want to present yourself as authoritative or approachable? Be careful not to sound preachy or officious—you don't want to turn away readers from the start. Write a few sample posts in

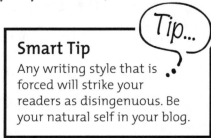

Smart Tip

Any writing style that is forced will strike your readers as disingenuous. Be your natural self in your blog.

a text editor. Choose the one with which you are most comfortable. You writing should sound natural to you.

Your first post should introduce yourself, explain your reasons for starting the blog, and announce your blog's purpose. Think about what your future readers, who will be coming back to read this post, will want to know. Include any credentials you may have on the topic, why you find the subject interesting, and what you hope to accomplish through blogging. Also try to include some fun personal notes, if appropriate, like the names of your pets or your other hobbies. Often readers like to know some personal details about the blogger they're reading.

First Months

The first four to eight weeks in the life of your blog are important. In this time you will learn a lot about your business, your blogging platform, and your audience. These will not be profitable weeks, but the content you create and the fine tuning you do will quickly prove valuable.

Filling Your Archive

Now that blogging is underway, it is time to get down to business. You should build up a few weeks of posts in your archive so that when readers do visit your blog, it doesn't appear to be a fly-by-night operation. These weeks are important as readers will be using the posts you make during this time to evaluate whether or not the content you're providing is worth their time. Most people, as you know, lead hectic lives. It is hard enough to capture a busy person's attention, let alone hold it for any amount of time. Spend considerable time ensuring the quality of what you write here.

Post to the blog with the regularity you expect to have once the blog is fully established. If you post too seldom because you spend too much time polishing your entries, your blog will appear to provide less than what you intend it to. If you post too often, with the idea that you should provide all you can as early as you can, you not only will run out of content to post fairly quickly, but once you slow the frequency of your posts, the readers that you have managed to attract will be let down. Instead of posting every idea you have when it strikes you, write them to separate list of future post ideas. If they don't contain time-sensitive content, meter posts to the blog over

Smart Tip

If you're excited to begin writing posts, you can begin writing and collecting content during your research for blog platforms. This will give you a head start once the blog platform is ready.

Tip...

time. So, for example, if you have 14 posts ready to go on Monday morning, don't post them all on Monday and Tuesday—leaving yourself nothing to post over the rest of the week. Meter out your content over time so that you have a consistent, predictable, publishing schedule. Your readers will appreciate the predicability.

Consistency

If you're considering seeking private sponsors for your site, these first weeks also set the theme of your site in the minds of potential advertisers. If you run a blog about the best window cleaning solutions but half your posts are about national politics because that's what has your attention this month, window cleaning companies will likely shy away from your blog because you shied away from the topic that sells their products. Stick to your topic, and keep your future sponsors in mind. Your readers will appreciate the consistency too.

Testing Your Platform

These first weeks provide you with a good opportunity to really test your blogging platform. You will want to be sure that everything is in working order before you begin inviting thousands of people to come see what you made. Check that the archive is archiving, that the friendly URLs are friendly, that the images load, that weblogs.com is notified, and that your posts appear in the format you intend. Invite your friends, with their different computers with different web browsers, to poke around the blog and report to you what they find.

Your testing friends may not find any software problems, but they will probably provide you with a useful end user point of view and comments such as, "I couldn't find the RSS feed link." Or, "How do I access the archive?" Make notes on what they find and improve your blog's performance and layout where you can.

If you've chosen to use a web-based service, you likely won't find any programming bugs (let alone ones that you can fix). But, now that you have content up, you should approach your blog from the reader's point of view and make sure that you have it set up in an easily navigable, attractive, and readable fashion.

If you have installed your own blogging application, use this time to test every function that a reader can use. Test the comments, the trackback, the search, and the archive. Click everywhere a reader can click and make sure that the links and features are working as expected.

Beware!
Building readership takes time. Don't expect the world to show up overnight. Hard work and patience will be important in the first months.

Generating Traffic

Attracting millions of readers may seem like a daunting task. A million people is an inconceivable number, let alone two or four million. Luckily, you aren't running for office and won't need to shake a million hands just to get people to read your blog. In fact, you will likely be able to count on one hand the number of readers you will run into over the life span of your blog. Another aspect of promotion that tends to scare people is the sheer number of web sites that advertise other web sites. How can you possibly contact them all? More good news: You don't need to. One wonderful thing about the internet is its high level of automation. There are services available to you that will make your job of directing internet traffic to your blog much easier than you might be thinking.

There are only a few ways that readers will ever find your blog—through search engines, blog directories, link exchanges, and word of mouth. Here are some thoughts on each of these avenues including the best ways to place your blog in front of the most potential readers.

Search Engines

The first order of business in promoting any site is letting the search engines know about it. Submitting your site to search engines simply alerts them to your presence. They will add your blog address to their web crawler queue, and eventually you'll be paid a visit by their web crawler robot for site scanning and potential indexing. Most top-level search engines would have found your site eventually anyway, so the only real advantage to submitting your link to them is that you give them a head start on finding you.

Search engines are tricky beasts. They are always evolving and changing the way they rank their search results. There is no way to guarantee that your blog will be at the top of any search results. In fact, there's no way to guarantee that your blog will be listed at all. Books, book series, and entire industries are devoted to the task of site search engine optimization, or SEO. Many companies have grown to be quite good at SEO, and could, no doubt, offer you a valuable service. This industry, however, is plagued with rip-off artists who take advantage of site owners' lack of technical know-how. You can submit your link to search

Beware!
If you choose to use an SEO service, read their references and resumes before you send the check. There are a few SEO scams that pose as legitimate companies.

engines yourself, at the links provided below. But if you're looking to have a professional do it for you, along with other optimization services, be sure to collect references before signing any contracts.

There simply is not room in this book to provide you with the all the knowledge and theory that goes into SEO. But here are the basics and the best things to do to increase your blog's chances of climbing the search engine results.

Submission Pages for Top Search Engines

- Google: www.google.com/addurl.html
- Lycos: www.lycos.com/addasite.html
- MSN: http://submitit.bcentral.com/msnsubmit.htm
- Yahoo! and DMOZ.org: Surf to appropriate category in their directories and click the "Submit Your Site" link at the very bottom.
- Note: The new Ask.com (formerly AskJeeves.com) does not accept link submissions and relies solely on their web crawlers to index sites.

Keyword Optimization

The concept of keywords is crucial to understand. Although they're moving away from it, many search engines still rely on the keyword concept for ranking. All of the contextual advertising programs you will use depend heavily on the keyword's presence on your blog. A keyword can be any textual word on your blog—words in images will not count. Search engine web crawlers and advertisement scripts collect all the words on your blog page and report them back to their respective services. The service, whether it is an advertising company or a search engine, then filters out all the words that are articles (the, an, a), quantifiers (all, few, many, etc.), and attributive adjectives (his, her, this, that, etc.). What's left are the nouns, pronouns, and meaningful adjectives that hopefully give an idea of what the scanned page is all about.

In the case of your blog, you will want to choose five or six words that accurately describe the content of your blog. Avoid adjectives such as "awesome," "killer," and yes, even "blogtastic." These will do little for you. You will likely be able to come up with far more than five or six, and in that case you should base keyword worth on two factors: word popularity, or the frequency that the word appears in search engine searches; and the word's profitability. Word popularity will help you get into more search engine search results; word profitability will help you make more money from advertisers.

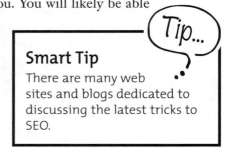

Smart Tip

There are many web sites and blogs dedicated to discussing the latest tricks to SEO.

Keyword Popularity

There are many tools on the internet to help you determine a word's popularity among search engine searches. If it is not clear to you that one word would be more popular than another that you've chosen, use these tools to help you decide between the two.

- Overture's Tool: http://inventory.overture.com/d/searchinventory/suggestion/
- Telepro's Google Tool: www.tele-pro.co.uk/scripts/google/popularity.asp
- SubmitExpress's Tool: www.submitexpress.com/keytracker.html

Keyword Profitability

Determining a word's profitability potential is less concrete. Think about potential items available that might be associated with the word in question. Say you run a blog that reviews digital music downloading services and are trying to decide between the popular keywords "MP3" and "iPod." "iPod" wins for the following reasons: MP3s are nothing more than a file format. Even though it is possible to purchase MP3 files, they rarely fetch more than one dollar, and therefore advertisers will not spend big money promoting the sale of MP3s alone. The iPod, however, fetches hundreds of dollars per sale, and is flying off the shelves. The competition in the iPod market is fierce and the item fetches a high price, so advertisers are willing to pay more per click to advertise their iPod stock over their competitors. This makes the word "iPod" more profitable for web site owners than "MP3" because ads for iPods pay more per click than ads for MP3 services. Pay-per-click is covered in more depth later in this chapter.

Of all the words that you originally came up with to describe your site, select just five or six based on their appropriateness, popularity, and profitability. These will be your site's keywords. Now, splash them around your blog. Always use the same five or six keywords, but do not overdo it, as these services that scan your blog are likely to block your site if they determine that you are "keyword bombing"—boosting your overall keyword ratio by placing them unnecessarily. But place a few in your blog title tag, on your About Me page, in your site description, in your posts and post titles when appropriate, in your friendly-URLs, and in the links on your site wherever you can manage. Both search engines and advertising networks give additional weight to keywords contained within links. This will help you achieve more effective results from both.

Of the two example links below, the second would be a more effective use of your "iPod"

> **Tip...**
>
> **Smart Tip**
> Keyword profitability is one factor used by professional bloggers when choosing a subject on which to base their blogs.

keyword. The "links" in the examples below are what we've underlined.

OK: "Check out our latest review of the 60 GB iPod <u>here</u>."

Much Better: "Check out our latest <u>review of the 60 GB iPod.</u>"

Search Engine Advertising

Another way to work your way onto the search engine result pages is to pay your way to the top. Top search engines, such as Google, Yahoo!, and Ask.com allow you to place an advertisement along the side, or across the top, of search results pages for related searches. This can be a great way to reach your target audience because your advertisement will only be shown to people who are searching for your content.

These ads systems, again, work on the keyword principle. Once you have applied, and been accepted, to the advertising program, you simply write out a very brief advertisement for your blog using the template provided. Then you place private bids for appropriate keywords in an ongoing Vickery auction. You will pay the search engine the amount of one bid increment above the second-highest bid every time any-one clicks on your advertisement. If you secure the highest bid, you win the right to have your ad display at the top of the paid advertisement bar shown for any searches that contain that keyword. This happens for a specified amount of time, or until you're bid off the page. If you have the second highest bid, your ad is listed in spot number two, and so on. Less than ten ads are shown on any given results page, so top spaces are limited for any one keyword.

You can have as many different keyword advertisements running at one time as your budget will allow. So if your blog is about collectible action figures, you would do well to secure a spot for your ad for keywords like "G.I. Joe" or "Superman" or "action figure." These key-words that you purchase should be related to, if not exactly, the keywords you chose earlier in this chapter.

Some of the most popular search engine advertising programs are:

* Google's AdWords: http://adwords. google.com

- Yahoo!'s Overture: http://www.over ture.com
- MSN adCenter: http://advertising.msn .com/msn-adcenter
- Ask.com's Sponsored Listings: http:// sponsoredlistings.ask.com/

Figures are according to Nielsen/Net Ratings, as of March 30, 2006.

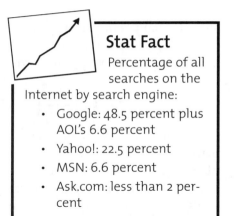

Stat Fact

Percentage of all searches on the Internet by search engine:

- Google: 48.5 percent plus AOL's 6.6 percent
- Yahoo!: 22.5 percent
- MSN: 6.6 percent
- Ask.com: less than 2 percent

These programs are a good way to draw in a lot of traffic relatively quickly. Research the different programs to find one that is right for you. We recommend joining at least Google's AdWords, as the service is very easy to use and Google commands the lion's share of search engine traffic.

In addition to these internet advertising programs, once you grow large enough you should consider real-world advertising. Placing advertisements in appropriate magazines, newspapers, and such can produce respectable results as well. Marketing of internet services should not be limited to the internet. When readers see ads for your blog in the real world, you gain a level of professionalism for which most blogs strive. Implement this strategy slowly to allow for careful monitoring. Sometimes, if advertisements are poorly worded, poorly designed, or just in the wrong magazine, the results won't justify the expense.

Blog Aggregators

A blog or news aggregator is a tool that retrieves RSS, Atom, or XML feeds from news sources, blogs, and other publishing platforms, and pulls them all together in one place. Aggregators are being integrated with a lot of internet-capable applications such as Firefox, Safari, Opera, and even iTunes. This allows these applications and aggregator web sites to list published information from all across the internet in one place—for example, in Firefox's dynamic bookmarks feature, or in iTunes's podcast feed directory. The use of aggregators that is most applicable to your needs is in the creation of online blog directories. Blog directories pull together billions of posts from millions of blogs and indexes, categorizes, and places them in an easily searchable database. Many visitors to these directories are looking for interesting blogs to read, and if yours is not among them, you lose readers.

I suggest enabling the RSS, Atom, or XML feed feature on your blogging platform and submitting it to all the aggregators you can find. For no extra work per post, you can make sure your blog is included in the search results of these popular tools. A few popular aggregator sites are profiled as follows, and several others to which you should submit your feed are also listed. In general, though, it is helpful to submit your feed to all the aggregators you come across.

Technorati

Stat Fact
Technorati claims to be tracking 32.5 million sites with 2.2 billion links, which, if you spend a few minutes browsing its directory, you'll soon believe.

Technorati is by far the largest blog aggregator on the internet. Start submitting your blog to directories here. They use a system that they call Technorati Tags to categorize the feeds they aggregate. It is not a proprietary system, but one that they've popularized. Technorati Tags' goal is to have every blog and every blog post tagged with a category. If your blogging platform supports post categories, and notification of Technorati of updates, you already take advantage of this system. If you are lacking one of these capabilities, Technorati has instructions on how to take part anyway.

Visiting the Technorati Tags web site (www.technorati.com/tags) will give you an idea of the intended goal and the power of this categorization system. When the 32.5 million blogs on Technorati send their categorized post notifications to the Technorati Tag system, the most popular post categories increase in font size, denoting their growth in popularity. For example, following the launch of Apple's iPod nano, the iPod tag quickly grew to dwarf out the Firefox, President Bush, and sex categories. By watching the popular post categories grow, move, and shrink, one can literally watch the conversations across the blogosphere evolve and change.

Participating in the Technorati Tag system will help you become a more involved member of the blogosphere and will place a link to every post you write on the Technorati web site, where it is searchable and previewed by the millions of Technorati users.

Tip...

Smart Tip
Blog aggregators can lead new readers to your blog, but don't rely solely on them for new traffic. Your posts will be listed in among billions of other posts, so you'll have plenty of competition.

blogexplosion

The blogexplosion service is a free blog aggregator and promotional community. It is mainly an online collection of bloggers who have joined blogexplosion in the hopes of finding readers for their blogs. The site features the usual featured blogs on the main page, the recently updated feature, and random member blog previews. But the community also has some fun ways to promote interaction amongst the bloggers in the community, such as Battle of the Blogs.

Battle of the Blogs is a fun way to pit your blog against someone else's in a custom challenge agreed to by both bloggers. Community credits are wagered and the blogging community reads the blogs over a period of time and votes on the winner of the particular challenge. It is a fun way to draw in traffic while building an active community. Visit the site at www.blog explosion.com.

Weblogs.com

Weblogs.com is a rather simple aggregator that consists of nothing more than a list of 100 recently updated blogs. It isn't particularly useful, as there is no search function or categorization of posts, and because the weblogs.com collection of blogs is so large that well over 100 blogs are updated simultaneously a new Top 100 is created every minute. That being said, it is popular, and most blogging platforms support notification of weblogs.com upon updating. So you might as well submit your feed here too. It's free.

Blogrolling.com

Blogrolling.com is an aggregator service that has been built to help bloggers maintain up-to-date blogrolls. A blogroll is a list of links to other blogs, and blog posts, in the sidebar of your blog. It is essentially your blog's honor roll, or a "I'll link you if you link me" party-in-a-sidebar. Usually to edit a blogroll, a blogger must edit the blog's template code. Blogroller.com aggregates the feeds from the various blogs of your choosing and updates the blogroll on your blog automatically. It's a fun tool. You should submit your link to them for possible inclusion into other blogger's blogrolls at www.blogrolling.com/ping.phtml.

Link Exchanges

The main goal of promoting your blog is to attract blog readers. And, where will you look for the highest percentage of blog readers? Why, other blogs of course! Swapping links with other bloggers is a great way to cast out a large net across the blogosphere and pull in a lot of readers. Blogger referrals of other bloggers has a high-percentage conversion rate

because readers most often trust that if their favorite blogger says something is interesting, it is. The exchange is done in three main places: blogrolls, trackback, and post links.

TrackBack

The technological aspect of TrackBack was explained briefly in Chapter 2. Here you'll learn how to use it to attract more readers. If you think of the blogosphere as a web of linked blogs, TrackBacks would be one of set of those links. Using TrackBacks is a great way to connect yourself to other blogs and to other blogs' readers.

If two blog platforms are both equipped with the TrackBack protocol, then they can exchange TrackBacks. A blog platform without the TrackBack protocol can neither send nor read TrackBack links. If your platform does not support the protocol, search for a plug-in that would give you the ability. If no such plug-in exists, you might consider switching to a platform with included support for the feature. TrackBack attracts readers in the following manner.

Alex, of cuteK9blog in Chapter 1, posts an article he's written about how he was able to cure his St. Bernard of slobbering. The article was well written and insightful. Duncan, a fellow blogger and St. Bernard owner, reads Alex's post and finds the information in it to be quite helpful, though somewhat incomplete. Duncan returns then to his own blog, SBA: St. Bernards Anonymous, and writes a post discussing Alex's article and adding the information he thought to be missing. Before publishing the post, Duncan returns to Alex's article and copies the provided TrackBack URL. He returns to his post-in-progress and pastes this URL into the TrackBack field. Duncan then inserts a regular link in his post's text to Alex's article and publishes the post.

Automatically and invisibly upon posting, Duncan's blogging platform sends a TrackBack ping to Alex's blogging platform notifying it that Duncan is discussing Alex's post on the SBA: St. Bernards Anonymous blog. Alex's blog automatically inserts a link to Duncan's new post underneath Alex's original article. Now the two blogs are reciprocally linked: Alex's TrackBack link to Duncan's blog, and Duncan's regular link to Alex's blog. This reciprocal link allows the readers of both blogs to track the same discussion across multiple blogs.

As you can see from this example, the more TrackBack links you set up, the more readers from other blogs you invite to your blog to discuss the same subject. Connect your blog to others with TrackBacks as often as you can. But don't be tempted to do so disingenuously. Other bloggers have a very low tolerance for spamming bloggers, or sploggers.

Blogrolls

Blogrolls are simply a list of links to other blogs that bloggers often display in their blog's sidebar. The criteria for being added to a blogroll is set by the blogroll's owner. Some bloggers create blogrolls based on geographic location and some on content similar to their blog. Sometimes a blogger will list her friends' blogs in her blogroll, or even just the blogs that she enjoys reading.

It will be worth your while to visit blogs that have content similar to yours, that are in—or about—your geographic location, or are even just the blogs of your friends and asking to be included in their blogrolls. Ask in private e-mail, and never in the comment section of the other person's blog. Also, aim high. There's no harm is asking high-profile blogs to include you in their blogrolls. Being linked from a well-regarded, high-traffic site will boost both your traffic and your credibility. If your request is accepted, you will often be asked to reciprocate the link in your own blogroll.

Blogrolling is a less-formal, nonautomated, less-purposed version of TrackBacks. So feel free to link any blogs you would like to in your own blogroll. You won't be violating any unwritten code of blogger etiquette by doing so. Just try to keep them organized in some sort of categorical way to make it easy on your reader. You may need to create more than one blogroll to accommodate all your various links.

Word of Mouth

Positive word-of-mouth promotion is a good friend to any business. Luckily, due to your business's operating environment (the internet), starting the word-of-mouth e-mail snowball is simple. An "e-mail this post to a friend" link is a simple, yet effective, tool. Most blog platforms include this feature already, but if not, you should edit your site's template to include such a link on every post. It will enable your readers to send a brief e-mail message right from your blog to all their friends. This e-mail just contains a simple note and a link to the post they're currently reading. Once the e-mail snowball has started rolling, it only takes a few minutes for it to potentially grow into an avalanche of traffic.

Beware!
Starting your own word-of-mouth campaign via email is hard to do successfully without crossing the line into SPAMming. If word-of-mouth doesn't take off initially, don't force it with more e-mails.

The real key to starting this word-of-mouth-traffic-avalanche is creating unique and interesting, or extremely useful, content. Nobody bothers to forward boring links to one another.

Generating Revenue

You should now have two of the three necessary ingredients in place for building a successfull blogging business: a steady stream of content and a good amount of traffic. The final ingredient is the integration of a revenue stream. Bloggers have found many ways to earn money with their blogs. Your chosen method, or combination of methods, should be appropriate for your intentions and content. For example, digital photography blogs have a hard time selling hats and t-shirts, while cartoon blogs can be rather successful at it.

The most proven methods in this chapter are outlined below. But don't limit your revenue solution to just these methods. You know your audience better than anyone else, and therefore know what they will want, and what they will reject. Don't be afraid to experiment with new methods of earning money or combining established methods. Perhaps you are a unique case and need a unique business model. Blogging as a business is a new concept, and therefore old business models may not always be the most effective ways to generate revenue. That said, here's a list of established methods that are currently working for professional bloggers.

- selling of merchandise with the blog's brand and content (books, hats, mugs, etc.)
- soliciting donations from your readers
- participating in affiliate programs
- selling paid memberships
- selling advertising space
- advertising another business (such as your web design) to your audience.

Consider each method and its appropriateness for your content and business model. Some, obviously, are more profitable than others. Information on these most reliably profitable methods follows.

Donations

As a general rule I do not recommend soliciting donations from your readers. It casts an unprofessional light on your blog. If you are providing a valuable service, you should be able to find revenue streams without resorting to charity. Relying on the charity of others is never seen as appropriate for a professional business. If you're aiming to become a top-earning professional blogger, donations will not get you there.

Donations do, however, have their place. If you are adverse to placing advertising on your blog due to moral, commercial, or even aesthetic objections, accepting donations can be a suitable alternative. You can avoid selling products for other people, subjecting your audience to ads, and it requires only a little button in one of your blog's sidebars.

The best way to go about accepting donations from your readers is to use the National Public Radio (NPR) model of fundraising. Instead of constantly hounding your readers for cash, hold fund drives for a week at a time, a few weeks per year. Devote the rest of your time to providing a quality service that your readers will be proud to support. Take down the donation button when you're not running a fund-drive, as it doesn't look professional. Instead, place a small text link at the bottom of your site where people can make donations between fund drives, and then restore the button once it is time for a fundraiser.

Be sure to announce when your fund drive is taking place a week or two before it begins. In your announcement, inform your readers when and why it is taking place and what you hope to collect. Clearly state the benefits that your service provides, and that in lieu of placing advertisements, you depend on reader support. Place a page on your site describing the details of the fund drive, and where the money that's donated is spent. Use percentages if you're shy about posting actual dollar amounts. Include on this page hosting fees, blogging service fees, ISP fees, and contributor fees—including yourself.

When the fundraising week begins, place a few posts every day reminding readers that you're holding your "Annual August Fund Drive" and that you would very much appreciate their support.

The old-fashioned method of receiving donations as a check or money order in the mail should be made available to readers who might be wary of conducting transactions online, but you should also sign up with an online financial service that makes it easy for readers to contribute with their credit or debit cards. There are many programs that allow you to do this— some are strictly set up for fundraising, some are

Smart Tip *Tip...*

A meter in your sidebar showing how much has been collected and how much farther you have to go to meet your goal is a great motivator for your reader to contribute. It's part of human nature to want to see those little thermometers pop.

⚠ **Beware!**
PayPal is not a bank, and therefore not FDIC insured. So it is possible that if PayPal goes belly-up, you would lose all the money in your account. You can "download" your balance to your local bank; get in the habit of doing that regularly.

part of a larger financial service. The ones profiled here are quite popular and trusted by millions of web site owners to handle their income.

PayPal

PayPal is the gold standard of online payment services. It functions very much like any local bank in that, once registered, you will have an account that allows you to deposit and withdraw money to and from other regular bank accounts. Paypal even offers money market services for higher interest rates, and a debit card with cash back rewards similar to a regular bank. However, Paypal is an internet-based company with no branches or ATMs. Its primary innovation, and reason for its success, was in creating the ability for people to easily send and receive money online. Anybody with a PayPal account can send money (from their PayPal account balance, linked credit cards, or linked bank accounts) to any person with an e-mail address. Although receiving the money requires signing up with PayPal and either requesting a check or "downloading" the money into your personal bank account.

PayPal quickly became popular as a tool to pay for items purchased on eBay and small retail web sites, because the company has developed powerful yet simple online payment tools for small businesses and organizations.

Once you register for a PayPal account, you will be able to create, through its "Accept Website Payments" wizard, a "Donate Now" button for your blog sidebar. The wizard produces code that you simply cut and paste into your sidebar template code. Visitors to your blog will be able to click on PayPal's "Donate Now" button, insert their credit or debit card information into PayPal's secure checkout, and submit their donation directly to your PayPal account. The money is instantly available to you. PayPal takes care of sending receipts, notifying you of the donation, and tracking payments you've received.

For this service you pay no monthly fee, no setup fees, and no terminal fees, like you would for a merchant account. PayPal charges per-transaction fees. To see the current fees that PayPal charges, go to their main site at www.paypal.com, scroll to the bottom, and click the "Fees" link. At the time of this printing, the current per transaction fees for receiving money are 1.9 to 2.9 percent depending on the amount, plus $0.30.

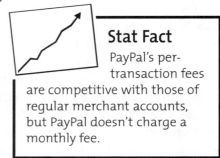

Stat Fact
PayPal's per-transaction fees are competitive with those of regular merchant accounts, but PayPal doesn't charge a monthly fee.

PayPal is a powerful system with many options for customization. For example, if you'd like to present your readers with some payment flexibility, you have the option to set up a button that accepts recurring payments, allowing your readers to spread out their donations over time. PayPal will automatically charge the user's card according to the schedule you set and dumps the money into your account.

PayPal can be a valuable service for you. For more information visit www.paypal.com.

Amazon Honor System

The Amazon Honor System was designed specifically for the task of enabling web site owners to collect donations for their frequenters. It works in much the same fashion as if you were to set up PayPal's donation button on your site. Your readers can submit money to you using their major credit cards through Amazon's own checkout system. The money is sent to you every 14 days, or whenever you request it, by direct deposit into a checking account.

After signing up with Honor System, you'll receive what Amazon calls a PayBox, which is really just code for a graphic that you cut and paste into your blog's sidebar—like PayPal's button. When visitors click the PayBox, they are sent to your Honor System PayPage that Amazon hosts for you. This PayPage is customizable—more so than PayPal's checkout page—and, if your readers happen to be Amazon.com customers, this page will greet them by name.

The Amazon Honor System does not charge any recurring fees. Instead they charge a per-transaction fee which is substantially higher than PayPal's—currently 15 percent of the total amount donated, plus $0.15. Paying Amazon 15 percent of your income may seem exorbitant, but it is a quality service and offers a lot of flexibility. For more information, visit http://honorsystem.amazon.com.

Click & Pledge

Click & Pledge is a service designed specifically with fundraisers in mind. It has been around since 2000, and has been making raising money online easier for charities, shelters, and organizations. It offers innovative tools such as virtual food drives, interactive "Click-It" donation buttons for your site, and those red contribution thermometers that everybody loves so much.

Some of these tools can be taken advantage of today by all bloggers. Some, unfortunately, like the contribution thermometer, require that you take advantage of its inhouse web site management service. Fortunately, it has seen the need for better off-site web site integration for campaigners who already have their own web sites and are in the process of launching a third version of its system that will include useful widgets that you can easily integrate into your blog.

Click & Pledge is a company devoted to helping you raise money. Like the other two services outlined, it does not charge recurring fees, only fees per transaction. Unlike PayPal or Amazon, it does not charge one rate for all transactions, rather it charges a different set rate for each different credit card system. American Express is the most expensive at 8.75 percent, while for MasterCard and Visa it charges 4.75 percent.

Because Click & Pledge is set up exclusively to facilitate fundraisers, it is able to offer advanced fundraising features. One such offering is the Empower program, wherein it advertises a product giveaway on your behalf, through your site. Contributors are entered into a drawing for the prize item, and then at the end of the fundraiser, a winner is picked. Click & Pledge sends off the item, and you collect for donations. Also, like PayPal, Click & Pledge offers the setup of recurring payments, giving you and your readers more options.

Click & Pledge provides wonderful support via telephone, e-mail, and live chat. If you ever have a question for the sales or support staff, visit their site, click the Live Chat button and you'll have your answer in seconds. You'll find this feature extremely useful if you decide to take advantage of its services. Visit the web site at www.click andpledge.com.

Affiliate Programs

Once you have substantial traffic, other companies will want to profit from it. This is the central idea directly behind affiliate programs, and, in a less direct way, advertising in general. Affiliate programs function basically like any other form of text or banner advertising, in that you are paid to place an advertisement for a service or company on your blog. They are different, and warrant their own section, because the theory behind when you deserve payment is different. Some ads you place on your site are passive—you get paid just for displaying them. Some ads you place on your site require action—you get paid only when your visitors click on that ad. (These differences are covered in more detail later in this chapter.) Affiliate program ads require not only that your visitors click an ad, but also a resulting sale. This is a long way from simply selling advertising space in the corner of your blog.

> **Beware!**
> Affiliate programs with unknown companies are often not lucrative. Search for programs with large retailers like Amazon, PC Connection, and eBay.

Unless your blog is specifically suited to an affiliate program format of profiting, this revenue stream will not be very effective for you. However, in specific cases, it could be. For example, if your blog discusses the latest best-selling mystery novels and your recommendations pull some weight with your readers,

> **Beware!**
>
> The farther from the source company that your advertising program gets, the smaller your percentage of the sale will be.

devoting a sidebar of your blog to the recommended novel with an Amazon.com Associates affiliate "Buy It Now" button may do very well for you. In this way, your blog would function as something of an Amazon outlet store. You would need a lot of visitors, and a lot of sales for the percentage you earn per sale to add up, but if you can beef up those two factors, this is a viable option.

Selling books is not your only option. There are thousands of affiliate programs offered by every size and type of online retailer. Even Amazon, as you probably know, offers a huge range of items—some of which may be suitable for you to sell from your blog, and for all of which Amazon will pay you a percentage of sales. If you think that the quasi-store blog format will work for your subject matter, do a quick search on Amazon to see if they offer appropriate items. Then, for a comparison, do a larger search on the internet to find any affiliate programs from sellers of similar items. You may find a better percentage per sale, and more flexibility in how you present their items on your blog.

If you can't find an appropriate individual retailer with an affiliate program, you could sign up with an affiliate marketing service. These services function similarly to the textual advertising networks in that they are the intermediaries for online retailers and advertisement publishers. Companies like LinkShare (www.linkshare.com), ClickBank (www.clickbank.com), and Commission Junction (www.cj.com) have large directories of retailers of all kinds who offer affiliate sales. For a percentage of these sales, these intermediaries will help you get set up with ads from retailers.

Merchandising

If you have blog content that lends itself to being printed on mugs and T-shirts and mousepads, you should consider selling branded merchandise from your blog. This method works particularly well with humor blogs, cartoon blogs, and the occasional political blogs. Not only is it extremely fun to see your brand printed on all sorts of swag, but it will help you with promotions, and earn you some money too.

There are several ways to go about creating and selling your own merchandise. The first, and most obvious, is to trek down to your local t-shirt shop with a copy of your logo and that funny quip you were up all night writing, hand them over, wait a few days, and then take home 12 boxes of polyester goodies. Displaying your new wares on your blog shouldn't be a problem, you just take a photo, price it, and place it alongside a PayPal "Buy It Now" button, which you can create easily after signing up for a PayPal Business account. PayPal also offers instant shopping carts for easy integration into any web site. It is a quick and easy way to get set up with full e-commerce on your blog.

If you would not like to depend solely on PayPal for your e-commerce needs, you could open an eBay Store, a Yahoo! Store, or you could install your own e-commerce application. To do the latter, you will need to have access to your web server, and install a separate shopping cart program alongside your blogging platform and then integrate it with a third-party payment processor and merchant account. This can be unnecessarily complicated for merchandisers just starting out. If you would like to test the merchandising waters, we suggest opening an account at one of the store services mentioned above. This way you can determine the profitability of merchandising without too much hassle.

The quickest route to selling branded merchandise is to sign up with an on-demand branding service. An on-demand branding service is an online store that sells a variety of items that are basically blank canvasses for your logo, brand, or funny quip. The various services available offer different items, such as mousepads, T-shirts, bumper stickers, clocks, aprons, baby jumpers, and so on. Each item you select to sell will be displayed, with your graphics on it, on the web page that the service provides you. Through this page, your readers can purchase items, which are then printed and shipped. You don't need to worry about doing anything except setting up the store and collecting the revenues. The service handles the rest.

The disadvantage of these services is that they keep a hefty percentage of the sale price. You will end up making only $2 to $6 per item, which, if you're selling hundreds of items, isn't a bad way to pad your income while filling the world with what are essentially promotional materials. Besides, if they are saving you time by buying the goods, branding the goods, selling the goods, and shipping the goods, they may be worth the cost.

We've listed the top on-demand branding services on page 61. Visit each service and read through their pricing policies—each one works a little differently. Also, the products that are available on each of these services varies greatly.

Be sure before you sign up that you will be able to sell the particular item you have in mind.

On-Demand Branding Services

- Zazzle: www.zazzle.com
- Branders: www.branders.com
- CafePress: www.cafepress.com

Memberships

A few blogs are switching to a pay-for-access membership business model. This is a relatively new experiment in the blogosphere and has yet to prove itself as either doomed or successful. The jury is still out on whether or not readers are willing to pay for the content of a particular blog, especially when a search on Technorati will likely produce many similar blogs covering similar topics. We don't suggest moving to a full-membership business model as a new blog, where you block off all your content from the non-paying public. It will only serve to alienate potential readers and create another barrier between your blog and your profits. Also, because the membership movement is still so young, we suggest you use more traditional methods of building profits, while waiting to see whether or not readers reject the membership idea.

While a full-membership model will hinder your blog's growth from the start, there are some variations on the model that are worth considering. Selling memberships that offer other types of premiums can be quite attractive to your reader—not to mention that the "member" concept creates an aura of exclusivity surrounding your blog. Here are some membership business models worth exploring.

Partial Access

Instead of restricting nonmembers from an entire blog, some bloggers are having luck with selling memberships to exclusive content, such as different categories of posts, search functions, the archives, etc. By keeping most of the content free for the public, but requiring membership for exclusive content, the bloggers are able to maintain unrestricted growth in traffic, while offering incentives to paying members. Plus by creating an exclusive section, and awarding some of your readers with the flattering title of "member," you create an artificial desire to belong to your readership.

> **⚠ Beware!**
> Keep in mind that, unless you can find a plug-in that provides these functions for your blogging platform, or your service provides them, it will be necessary for you to do a little programming to implement them.

> ## ⚠ Beware!
> The Early Edition method requires programming, a plug-in, or built-in functionality to be viable. Manually posting content twice in two different parts of your blog isn't sustainable.

If you provide quality content and valuable incentives for membership at a reasonable price, this method will work well for you.

Early Edition

Another strategy some bloggers are testing out is the concept of early editions of posts. Paying members are able to log into the blog and read your posts several hours (or days) before they are automatically made available to the general readership. This method not only allows blog members to read posts before everyone else, but also to submit to the post comments first, participate in discussions earlier, and so on.

This is an easy method to run once it is set up because it does not require you to do anything above and beyond what you have been doing all along. This is just a method of metering out your content in such a way that it creates premium content out of the same old stuff.

Ad-Free Version

Perhaps the most successful membership strategy is selling an advertisement-free version of your site. This strategy is successful because it isn't based on exclusion and holding content ransom, which can annoy some readers. This, in fact, isn't a strategy at all. It is simply offering the service of an ad-free blog to readers who are willing to pay for it. Your blog remains the same for the public, but is improved for the ad-averse crowd.

Readers who don't mind reading advertisements aren't affected by this membership method at all. Their blog remains the same blog that they've always loved, without excluding them from features or content. And because they are happy to put up with your ads, you earn revenue from both the general public and from your paying members.

• • •

These membership methods do not need to be exclusive of one another. Many bloggers offer both ad-free versions of their blogs, and early editions of their posts. Fiddle with these methods and find the most profitable combination. Just don't fiddle so much that you annoy your readership. And, don't be afraid to ask them directly if they would be willing to pay for

> ## ⚠ Beware!
> The Ad-Free Method requires some extensive setup. Ask your blog provider the best way to go about setting this up for your particular situation.

an ad-free version, early posts, or exclusive content. The more research you do, the better your experiment will fare.

Selling Space to Advertisers

The standard and most reliable way to earn profits from your blog is by selling advertising space. Advertisers will pay good money to place their products on your site if the conditions are right. In order to be desirable to advertisers, your blog must have reliable traffic and content that's relevant to the advertiser's product or service. Most text ad networks take care of the latter for you by scanning your site text for keywords and displaying relevant ads, as we explained earlier. But signing up with contextual ad networks is not all there is to blog advertising. While getting the blog started, signing up with Google's AdSense just to get some money flowing is a good idea. But once you're established, if you're looking to make even better money with your blog, you'll need to go a few steps farther.

In this chapter I'll discuss the options you have when selling advertising space and provide tips for making the most of it. Consider how you can make best use of the following advertising options—each will require fine tuning down the road.

Ad Networks

The invention of the automated advertising network was a boon to the online advertising industry. It not only simplified the process for advertisers seeking exposure, it made the process a lot less painful for web site publishers as well. No longer was the lengthy and arduous task of seeking out private sponsors the only option for advertising income. Now, with a few simple lines of code, every web site on the internet could display six ads at a time that rotated automatically, updated as necessary, *and* were always relevant!

Advertising networks have been on the internet since the beginning. But the breakthrough of relevant textual advertising created a spike in the number of ad networks available to bloggers and web site publishers. You will have plenty of options when seeking a network to join. They all function similarly in terms of how they publish advertisements on your site. But, they all have different methods for how they pay, when they pay, and how much they pay.

CPC *vs.* CPM

Before you begin researching ad networks, you should be familiar with the difference between cost-per-click (CPC) advertising and cost-per-thousand (CPM)

> **Beware!**
> Entire books have been written about CPC advertising. If this is your chosen route, invest some time and money into additional research.

advertising. That their acronyms start with CP are the only things that are similar about the two pricing methods.

CPC advertising networks pay you some small amount of money every time a visitor to your site clicks on one of the advertisements you display for them. This amount of money will be unknown to you as it is worked out between the advertiser and the ad network and is different for each ad shown. You, obviously, will ultimately learn what you earned per click in your daily reporting statistics, but it will not be available to you beforehand, as the ads are served on your site in real time. The only way to increase your per-click revenue is through keyword optimization, which is covered later in this chapter.

Now, for example, if you run a blog about the latest in sneakers which serves up 500,000 ads per day, and your ad network displays a constant flow of ads for the latest sneakers, chances are that you will have a high conversion rate (ads clicked / total ads served) and do fairly well. Though if, for some reason, not one of your visitors is compelled to click on any of the 500,000 ads, you make no money—even though your site has been promoting the advertisers' goods all day long.

Serving thousands of ads and earning nothing (or little) may seem like a bum deal, and many would agree with you. The largest complaint about CPC programs is that often the conversion rate, on which you depend for revenue, hinges on factors beyond your control. If an advertisement contains errors, is unattractive, or is simply written in a noncompelling manner, your revenue will suffer.

The other method that ad networks use, CPM, is not based on conversion rates at all. In fact, no conversion is necessary for you to profit. This method is a more traditional approach to advertising revenue models in that advertisers pay web site publishers some amount of money for every 1,000 ads displayed on their web sites—whether those ads receive clicks or not. This can be a more reliable and predictable approach to collecting ad revenue because it is not based on factors beyond your control. It is simply based on your blog's traffic.

The overwhelming majority of ad networks use one of these two methods, and both have their advantages. But the advantages of each cannot be universally applied to all blogs.

For example, CPC advertisements work best on blogs that deal in subjects concerning hot commodity items: iPods, laptops, high fashion, etc. This is due to a number of reasons. First, advertisers are willing to pay a high-price

> **Beware!**
> CPM campaigns are not suited to blogs when just starting out. You will need to establish many thousands of visitors per day before this is a lucrative option.

per-click to display their ads because of the fierce competition in their market and the high prices that their items fetch. Second, people are willing to shop for and, usually, purchase these items online. These are specialty items that often cannot be purchased, or researched well, locally. Therefore these ads enjoy a high click-through percentage.

> **Beware!**
> Factor in your keyword profitability when choosing between CPC or CPM campaigns. If you have low chances for keyword profitability, choose CPM.

CPC ads do not work as well on all sites. Political blogs, for example, receive more traffic than most blogs out there. But, the keywords associated with political blogs (liberal, conservative, pinhead, moron) have a hard time selling tangible products. Therefore, CPM ads will work better for this given subject matter because they pay well on any site with high traffic.

Optimizing Layout

If you're looking to earn a living from blogging, you'll need to become familiar with the science behind visitor behavior and the psychology behind advertisement effectiveness and how it relates to online content. This will require some experimenting and data analysis. It sounds complicated, but in essence it is just the repeated process of tweaking some things and taking notes.

Success with any ad network is based on many factors. The amount you earn largely depends on your willingness to experiment with these factors, as they directly affect your monthly conversion rate. Simply plopping ads on your site will not be enough to maximize your generated revenue. You've got to tweak and test several factors including: keywords used in your posts or on your pages; placement of advertisements on your pages; and the color, size, and layout of ads—if your ad network allows you to change them.

> **Tip...**
>
> **Smart Tip**
> Often in CPM campaigns advertisers will need to approve your blog before you can display their ads. They don't want their vacuum cleaner advertisements appearing on a blog about the latest PHP/MySQL developments.

When tweaking, change one aspect of your advertising set up each week, whether it's ad color, placement, or keywords. Track your earnings for that week, and make adjustments accordingly. You may find that blue ads sell better than red ads, and that ads on the left sidebar sell better than ads across the top of the page. So, placing blue ads on the left sidebar will earn you the most revenue for those two factors. Once you have tested every factor you can think of, you will have the information necessary to put together the most effective ad layout for your blog.

Unfortunately, your "most effective layout" will inevitably lose effectiveness as your blog's readers get used to your layout and are able to visually gloss over those sections they know to contain ads. At this point you will have to test and reformat again. Once you go through this process three times, you will have the layouts for three highly effective advertising layouts on your blog. When you find your conversion rate dropping again, revert to the first highly effective layout that you used and cycle through your pre-made layouts when necessary.

Profiles of Ad Networks

There are many popular ad networks available to you. This section profiles the ones that bloggers report to work best for them. It is important to be happy with the ad network you join. It can make your business easy, or miserable depending on how it performs for you. They all offer different features; some may have what you're looking for, and some may not. It's important to find the one that best fits your needs. So read the profiles here, and visit each service's web site for more indepth answers to your questions. Each ad network below is a quality service.

Google AdSense

Google's AdSense is by far the largest and most well-known advertising network. When it first launched it was just a tool to help advertisers place ads alongside Google's own search results, but it has since been expanded to help advertisers place their ads on AOL, About.com, Amazon, Ask.com, Lycos, and any of the thousands of member sites of Google's AdWords program. It has the most reach of any network of its kind, and therefore it has the most participating advertisers—which translates into more chances for finding relevant content for you blog.

To say that the Google AdSense program works similarly to the others would be true, but it wouldn't give AdWords proper credit as the pioneer and standard of this industry. Most ad networks are patterned after the example AdWords sets, not the other way around.

Registration for AdSense is not difficult, but it requires that you provide your home address, contact information, and tax information. They will walk you through the whole process, and provide you information about off-site links where you can get the tax form that you'll need to submit to them. AdSense pays advertisement

Beware!
Some blog services do not allow Google AdSense to be used because they offer their own alternative ad service.

publishers every month via electronic funds transfer or a check mailed to the address you submitted during application. For security purposes, AdSense will not allow you to change your address once it is submitted. You will need to close your account and reopen one with the new address if you move. This can be a pain, but well worth it if it means that your checks continue to flow, and arrive safely.

After your account is set up you will choose the sort of ads you would like to display on your site. You can choose between text ads or image ads, CPC ads or CPM ads. Both text and image ads can be paid on either a CPC or CPM basis. One restriction to keep in mind is that if you choose to display CPM ads, your site will need to be approved—based on your content—by the individual advertisers of each ad. This can severely decrease the number and rotation of ads that show on your site, but image ads may attract more clicks as they command more attention—which may be a good or bad thing to your readers.

Once you've selected your ad configuration, AdWords will provide you with a snippet of customized JavaScript code for you to include somewhere in your blog template code. Wherever you place this code, AdWords will display your new ads. You'll begin earning right away.

Once your account has earned at least $50, AdWords will mail a PIN code to the address you've used to register with the program. Upon receipt, you enter the PIN code only once to verify your mailing address is actually one to which you have access. When your account earns at least $100, you are eligible to receive a check for the full amount in your account when next they mail out payment checks or initiate funds transfers. Funds are disbursed approximately two weeks after the end of the month in which your account topped $100. If you are headed to Fiji on vacation and would prefer that AdSense hold your payment while you're away, they are happy to do that for you. Just let them know in your account settings.

AdSense reporting tools, like on any Google service, go above and beyond when it comes to providing you with useful information. On your main AdSense account page you'll see an overview of the day's earnings, page impressions, clicks, clickthrough rate, and clicks-per-thousand ads served. Moving into the Advanced Reports section gives you a chance to see more

Smart Tip *Tip...*
For even more usable information about your AdSense traffic, check out Google's Analytics program. This powerful site traffic reporting tool can be integrated with all your Google AdSense statistics for one very robust audience reporting system.

indepth information about the performance of your ads. And the Payment History page will show you every click clicked and penny pinched.

As every advertisement that AdSense serves is highly targeted to specific keywords, it is entirely possible that the ads served on your site could come from your competitors. For example, if you run a blog discussing the World Cup, then likely, through the course of natural discussion, the words "soccer," "World Cup," and "community" will be prevalent on your site. Now, because your site dominates the traffic for World Cup blogs, your closest competitor has signed up with Google AdWords to try to drum up some traffic of his own. But because he has a similar site and similar audience, he has indicated that his ads should show up on sites that are heavy in the words "soccer," "World Cup," and "community." This makes it very likely that you'll end up, at some point, in the undesirable position of showing ads for your competition on your site. Luckily, Google anticipated this being a problem and has provided you with the ability to block ads to competitors, simply by supplying their URLs in your AdSense preferences.

In the event that AdSense cannot find a relevant ad to display on your blog, they have a cache of public service announcements from which they pull. When AdSense displays a public service announcement (PSA), you receive no payment when a visitor clicks on it. And while it may contribute to the common good to load PSAs on your web site, it won't do much for your profits. If you find that your site is loading an inordinate number of PSAs, you should fiddle with the keywords you use in your posts and on your pages. Try to use more specific terms that people are more likely to search for online. For example, instead of writing "I got an awesome new pair of shoes!" try "I got an awesome new pair of Reebok sneakers!" People are more likely to search for "Reebok" than "shoes," and therefore that's the keyword on which advertisers are looking to focus. This places more ads on your site at more money per click.

After reworking your keywords, you will still see the occasional PSA loaded on your site. To allow you to make the most of the space on your blog, AdSense allows you to provide them with alternate content to load instead of PSAs. This content can be images, text, or even other paying advertisements for your private sponsors. If requested, AdSense will load this alternate content every time it can't find a relevant ad to load.

There are many independent reviews of AdSense published around the internet, and many of them praise the network for generating more ad revenue for web site owners than they originally thought possible. Of course, success with AdSense is based on many factors,

> **⚠ Beware!**
> There are many offers on the internet for programs or materials that claim to provide you with the secrets to instantly making millions with Google AdSense. These offers are both enticing and highly suspicious. Beware of scams.

including the few touched on earlier. Google provides some fantastic optimization tips in the Demos & Guides section of their AdSense Help Center at www.google.com/support/adsense. If you're considering AdSense, I suggest you watch its demos and read through its guides to make the most of your advertising.

For more information about AdSense in general, Google provides a tour at their web site: www.google.com/adsense. I recommend getting your feet wet with AdSense. It is a great program for beginners because it is quick to set up, free to join, and does not require minimum site traffic levels.

CrispAds

CrispAds is a blog-specific CPC advertising network. On the surface it functions similarly to AdSense: you register as a publisher, and after installing a snippet of code, you will display rotating text or graphic ads on your blog.

This where the similarity ends. CrispAds offers three ways to find advertisers for your site. The first is by signing up to display rotating, keyword-targeted, text ads. These ads, unlike with most text ad networks, are not determined by an automated keyword crawler that scans your blog for content. Instead, CrispAds asks you to select the keywords you would like to describe your blog, and ads that target to those keywords will be shown. This can help or hurt you, depending on your point of view.

On the one hand, selecting keywords to define your blog topic will keep your advertising focused on the general content of your site no matter what words the current post or discussion contains. On the other hand, these ads will not always be relevant to the topic being discussed on the page. They could help or hurt you depending on the specific topic of conversation.

For example, it is possible that the discussion on your digital photography blog will turn to iPods. Where automated, relevant, advertising would begin displaying ads for iPods during this discussion and likely translate into a spike in ad clicks, CrispAds will continue to show ads relevant to digital photography and you'll likely only maintain your average conversion rate. However, if the conversation drifts the other way—into a topic with little or no commercial keyword value—serving more digital photography ads will benefit you more than PSAs.

Another aspect to CrispAds that makes it different than most other ad networks is that they pay a standard $.20 per click on text ads. For most ad networks, this price is variable and dependent on the price that the advertiser is willing to pay per click. Usually the ad network

> **Tip...**
>
> **Smart Tip**
> When asked to define keywords for CrispAds, provide your keywords that have the highest profit potential.

69

takes a set percentage, and passes the rest along to you. CrispAds reverses that model and pays you a set amount, and takes what's left over. This, again, could be a good or bad thing.

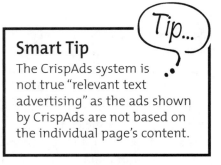
Monthly revenue forecasting is made much easier if you know the amount you earn for each click you produce. You would simply need to multiply your forecasted traffic by your average conversion rate by the $.20. Knowing about what you plan to earn in the following months will help you budget accordingly.

Also, while you often earn more than $.20 per click with other ad networks, you also often earn far less. Twenty cents is a respectable amount.

The second method CrispAds offers is monthly sponsorship. If you choose, you can submit your blog to their catalog, which will then be shopped around to their various advertisers. If selected by an advertiser, your blog will display ads from that one advertiser for a month. The pay for this sponsorship varies.

The third method available is to display rotating image ads based on the same keyword system that they employ for their text ads. Instead of a set $.20 pay out, these ads pay 70 percent of the total revenue they generate. So, if the advertiser is willing to pay CrispAds $1 per click, you take $.70. Because they host fewer image ads than text ads, it is possible that, once in a while, CrispAds will not be able to deliver image ads for the keywords you've selected. In this case, CrispAds will deliver appropriate text ads instead and you will collect the standard $.20 per click.

One small, but clear, advantage CrispAds has over AdSense is that they're willing to send payment for any amount over $5, as opposed to AdSense's $100 minimum. This will be helpful for bloggers who are just getting started and would really like to make use of that $95 sitting in their accounts. CrispAds pays on, or before, the 7th of every month. If your balance is less than $500, CrispAds pays only to a PayPal account. If you balance exceeds $500, you have the option of collecting payment via PayPal or check. For more information about CrispAds, visit their web site at www.crispads.com.

Pheedo

Pheedo is another blog-specific advertising network. It offers text ads through CPC and what they call flat-rate campaigns. They have no minimum traffic requirements so you can sign up as soon as you get started blogging, and like CrispAds, they do not use automated keyword crawlers to determine what ads are placed on your site.

Beware!

Choosing individual ads to display can be time consuming.

Unlike CrispAds, however, you do not select individual keywords to determine which ads are displayed. You directly choose the ads to display. This has the same drawbacks of CrispAds's method, but goes even farther toward ensuring that irrelevant ads are never shown on your site.

Pheedo pays 65 percent of all advertising revenue that your site generates for Pheedo. This means that the amount per click that you earn is variable and dependent on how much the advertiser pays Pheedo per click. This could mean either huge revenues or a pittance, depending on the ads you select.

Pheedo pays every 30 days, via PayPal or check, to all account holders who have accumulated a balance of $1 or more. This means that you will have no more need to anxiously watch the mail slot for those $101 checks. For more information about Pheedo's services, visit www.pheedo.com.

> ## Smart Tip
>
> An advantage that Pheedo offers over the other services is extensive RSS advertising integration. By placing your ads in your RSS feeds, you are able to recapture the advertising revenue that an ad-free RSS feeds normally sacrifice. This solves the problem of giving away your valuable content to those who are most interested in seeing it continue, your faithful feed subscribers.

BrightAds

BrightAds, by Kanoodle, is not a blog-specific advertiser. The service is available to all web sites, and therefore, given its larger reach, it has a larger advertising base. It was founded in 1999 as one of the first sponsored link advertising companies.

BrightAds serves relevant text ads on a rotating basis. It uses the CrispAds method of ensuring general blog relevancy by asking you to select keywords that pertain to your blog's subject. As noted above, this has pros and cons. All its ads are CPC, or, as they call it, RPC for "revenue per click." It offers the lowest per-click percentage of the services we feature at only 50 percent of the revenue that the ads on your blog generate.

BrightAds pays on a NET 30 days schedule on accounts that have earned $50 or more. For example, you will be paid August's earnings 30 days after the last day in August. You will be paid via check for the first 90 days, after which you will have the option of switching to payment through PayPal.

> ## Beware!
> Readers tend to think poorly of blogs that rely on invisible and somewhat invasive methods of profiting.

Like Pheedo, BrightAds offers RSS advertising, but they also offer a few more aggressive services not commonly available through other services. If you would like to earn revenue on

<table>
<tr><td>

Beware!

The advantage of earning revenue from every visitor may quickly be trumped by the price of annoying your readers. Pop-ups are pure evil. Pop-unders are less so, but still considered underhanded by the greater internet population.

</td></tr>
</table>

your site without displaying any ads at all, you can sign up for BrightAds Cookies. This service requires that you add a snippet of code to your web site which plants a cookie—or tiny file of information—into the user's web browser. This file will contain information about the user's surfing history and when he stumbles upon another web site in the Kanoodle network, tailored ads will be shown to this user based on his surfing history. If the user then clicks on one of these tailored ads, you will receive a small portion of the pay-per-click price. BrightAds is willing to pay you to help further tailor its ads for its customers.

Another service it offers is BrightAds Pops—and yes, that means what you think it does. This service displays pop-under advertisements that load beneath your readers' browser windows every time they visit your blog. This is not a CPC program as you get paid for every ad shown, not every ad clicked. So, when your readers discover that—lo and behold—there's an advertisement under their browser, and quickly close it, you still get paid.

This has the benefit of paying you every time any visitor comes to your site. However, the payments will not be nearly as high as CPC rates, as advertisers will not want to pay you $.20 for your 500,000 visitors per month. Expect rates closer to $.01 or less.

If you decided to take advantage of BrightAds Pops, plan to do so on an experimental basis only. After implementing the pop-unders, watch your site traffic carefully. If it starts to nose dive you will need to yank the ads and then try to make amends with your remaining readers.

• • •

There are too many ad networks available to cover them all in detail. Beyond the standards covered above, there are still many to be explored, with even more features and innovations. Here is a list of some other advertising networks to research.

Adbrite: www.adbrite.com

Adgenta: www.adgenta.com

AdHearUs: www.adhearus.org

Adknowledge: www.adknowledge.com

AVN Ads: www.avnads.com

Bidvertiser: www.bidvertiser.com

Chitika's eMiniMalls: www.chitika.com

Clicksor: www.clicksor.com

DoubleClick: www.doubleclick.com

Fastclick: www.fastclick.com

Industry Brains: www.industrybrains.com

IntelliTXT: www.vibrantmedia.com

OneMonkey: www.onemonkey.com

Peak Click: www.peakclick.com

RevenuePilot: www.revenuepilot.com

SearchFeed: www.searchfeed.com

Target Point: http://publisher.targetpoint.com

TextAds: www.textads.biz

Text Link Ads: www.text-link-ads.com

Tribal Fusion: www.tribalfusion.com

Value Click: www.valueclickmedia.com

YesAdvertising: www.yesadvertising.com

Private Sponsors

The most profitable blogs use private sponsors instead of, or in addition to, their other revenue streams. This is where the big money lives, and it will be entirely up to you to go out and get it. As you saw above, the other methods of selling ad space rarely offer an exciting profit margin. Affiliate ads offer in the range of 10 percent per sale, and ad networks offer only between 50 and 65 percent. By cutting out the middleperson, you keep 100 percent of the revenue you generate. You are no longer depending on other services to provide your profits, and no longer need to stick to their policies and payment schedules. Remember, this is your business. You are offering a valuable service to both your readers and to your advertisers. You should have a say in how, when, and how much it will cost to connect those two groups.

The problem is: you need to do the work. You can read here how to go about it, but unfortunately, only you can make the phone calls, prepare the materials, sell the ad space, and invoice the advertisers. So take notes on this section keeping in mind that private sponsorships should be your goal. It will take some time for you to build your blog traffic and credibility and professionalism to a point where advertisers will consider you an effective direct avenue for their sales dollars. Use the

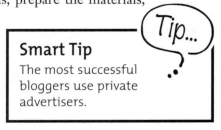

Smart Tip

The most successful bloggers use private advertisers.

alternative methods above until you really get rolling. Then begin to research possible companies that might be interested in striking a deal with you. You'll hear a lot of rejections, but the affirmatives will make it worth it.

The Media Kit

In order to sell advertising on your own, you will need to specify and quantify exactly what it is that you're selling. This information takes the shape of your blog's media kit. This document is vital to selling ad space to businesses. It presents all the data that a business will need to know about your blog, your audience, your traffic, and your offer.

Describe Your Blog

The first part of your media kit—your blog description—is the easy part. In this first section you simply describe your blog and the topics it covers. Provide some background information about why you started the blog, company milestones, and any awards or honors you've received along the way. Present yourself as a company, not as a blogger. Most businesses want to see what you do as a new form of traditional magazine or periodical.

Audience

The next section, your audience, is a little bit trickier to compile, and it will take a fair amount of time. Advertising businesses need to know exactly who their ads are reaching. They won't spend any money with you if can't prove that you have an audience for their product. So it is in your best interest to collect all the information you can about the people who come to your blog.

To collect information you will need to perform a survey of your readers. This data will need to be as unbiased as possible and draw from multiple cross sections of your readers. For example, if you perform your survey with 50 of your readers between the hours of 1 A.M. and 3 A.M., sure you'll have 50 surveys in the bag, but you'll have no idea what your daytime readers are like.

Here are some factors that businesses will be looking to learn.

- *Age*. Age ranges are preferable. Presenting just the average age of your readers doesn't provide advertisers with much useful information. It is more useful for

Smart Tip

Common interest and a sense of community isn't enough to sell advertisers on the idea that your site will sell their products.

them to know, for example, that 18 percent of your readers are 18 to 25, 60 percent are 26 to 35, 10 percent are 36 to 45, and so on.

- *Gender*. Percentage male, percentage female.
- *Location*. If you have a largely international audience, ask for countries. If most of your readers are from the United States, collect state data.
- *Occupation*. Occupational industries is preferable to user supplied data. Everyone has a different title, and learning that some of your readers are "Consultants" isn't helpful. Use, instead, categories like education, manufacturing, health care, communications, finance, retail, food service, etc.
- *Annual salary*. $10,000 to $20,000; $21,000 to $30,000, $31,000 to $40,000, and so on.
- *Time spent online*. Up to one hour per day, one to two hours, two to three hours, etc.
- *Role in purchasing at work*. This determines for the advertisers if there is a potential business market among your audience. If they can advertise to business decision makers, they want to know. Your categories can include "No influence, Valued Opinion, Recommend, and Decision Maker."
- *Size of employer*. This gives advertisers a glimpse into the nature of your work and position in the company. Decision Makers at 50,000-person companies tend to have larger budgets than those at five-person companies. It isn't a good or bad thing to have an audience full of either. It just helps advertisers decide if your audience is right for their service. Use brackets under 10, 11–50, 51–150, 151–350, 351–600, 601–1,000, 1,001–5,000, 5,001–10K, 10K and up.
- *Company annual revenue*. Again, this gives potential advertisers a glimpse into the available spending capital under the influence of the crowd they're marketing to.
- *Company spending*. This is not an amount, but rather a type of spending. Does your company purchase $1 million per year in rubber stamps, or in CPUs?
- *Type of personal spending*. This data is important because it describes where your audience's personal discretionary spending goes. Businesses will use this factor to decide whether or not advertising on your blog will be effective. Again, use categories, such as technology, sporting goods, media entertainment, etc.
- *Number of children, if any*. Advertisers want to know if your audience contains parents. Parents are a market unto themselves. Bachelors tend not to buy diapers, mini-vans, or pacifiers.
- *Size of household*. The number of people in any given household clues advertisers in to the number of people your targeted audience member have influence over. Plus, if you have 16 people in your household, it opens up the unique opportunity to advertise ear plugs, closet organizers, and toilet tissue.

These questions are just a few examples. You should include more that try to extract useable data from your audience. But keep in mind that your readers will not

▲

Smart Tip Tip...

Consider also offering something in return for submitting a survey. It could be a free hat, a free membership, or a free iPod if you want plenty of responses.

want to sit through a 30-minute survey. You'll end up with a lot of unfinished responses. If you have more questions than you can squeeze into a reasonable amount of time, separate the questions and perform multiple surveys over the course of several months.

There are several ways to perform a survey. We recommend enlisting the help of a professional surveying company. Collecting 50,000 surveys, analyzing the data, and pulling it all together in some sort of cohesive form is a Herculean task. It will take up all your time and drive you crazy. These services have tools specifically designed to perform this task and can do more, more effectively, than any individual could with years to prepare.

Here are a few survey companies to consider:

- SurveyMonkey: www.surveymonkey.com
- Vista Online Surverys: www.vanguardsw.com/vista/
- QuestionPro: www.questionpro.com
- SurveyGold: www.surveygold.com
- WebSurveyor: www.websurveyor.com
- Zoomerang: http://info.zoomerang.com

Once you have your data collected, you should put it together in an easily readable, attractive format.

Traffic Level

Now that you've established what your blog is, and who the people are in your audience, it is time to show how often your audience shows up. The third section of your media kit is devoted to your traffic levels.

Your site should have all along been automatically collecting more traffic data than you can ever hope to understand. This is a standard feature with most third-party web hosting services, but if you host your own server, or if you use a web-based blogging service, you might need to enlist the aid of a traffic reporting service. These traffic reporting services simply monitor all the traffic that comes to your site

Smart Tip Tip...

If presented in its raw format, traffic logs will just look like indecipherable server vomit. Be sure before you sign on with a particular traffic service that they present the data they collect in a meaningful and useful way.

and keeps records about who is visiting, from where, at what times, and for what content. If presented correctly, this can be extremely helpful and interesting information.

Some traffic monitoring services to consider:

- DeepMetrix: www.deepmetrix.com
- StatCounter: www.statcounter.com
- WebSideStory: www.websidestory.com
- Google Analytics: www.google.com/analytics/
- Omniture: www.omniture.com
- ClickTracks: www.clicktracks.com

Once you have compiled a few months worth of traffic reporting, you should compile it into your media kit in an easy-to-access format. Use charts and graphs. Use color. You should include such traffic statistics as overall page impressions per day/week/month, unique visitors per day/week/month, average time visitor spends on your blog, average number of pages viewed by visitors per visit, hourly usage, usage on days of the week, and anything else you deem useful. If you have statistics about how your ads from other sources have performed, include those numbers as well—conversion rate, click-through rate, impressions per month, and so on.

The Offer

The final piece of your media kit is your offer. This is a summary of what you've displayed in the previous pages and what exactly you're offering to the advertiser at what price. Remember, you're selling a service here. You set the price and the deliverables.

In defining your deliverables, detail how many ads you will show per page, and in which high-traffic locations. Make clear how many ads you expect will be shown over the course of a month. In setting a price, bloggers usually use the CPM method of pricing. Set a price per-thousand-ads shown and offer an upper limit to the client in case your monthly traffic levels go through the roof. Another, and easier, option is to offer a set price for a month of advertising, independent of traffic levels.

If you decide to sell advertising space on a per-month basis, take orders well in advance of when you need to. Book space for August in April if you can. This will give you plenty of time to coordinate ads and graphics and payment before it comes time to switch over all the ads on your site. Hopefully this schedule will give you an opportunity to book September, December, and so on before you're stuck with a month with no private sponsor.

> **Tip...**
>
> **Smart Tip**
> Pay-Per-Month advertising contracts guarantee income for you, and a price for the advertiser.

Tip...

Be open to negotiation, but go into the meeting knowing your bottom limit. You don't want to sell advertising space on your blog to private sponsors if you can make more with that space using the CPC and CPM ad networks.

Whatever payment method you choose, CPM or monthly, have a contract prepared and ready to sign. The advertiser will likely take the time to look it over and make suggestions, but have it ready for them to do so. A fair and common payment schedule to include in the contract for this type of monthly advertising is 50 percent of the contract up front to secure the spot in your schedule, and 50 percent upon the month's end. Taking in half payment up front provides a nice cash cushion, which makes budgeting easier.

Your ultimate goal should be to enlist private sponsors as clients of your blog and use them in addition to some ad network advertising, all while doing a little merchandising and possibly some memberships. You will need to test each of these methods and then tweak them for maximum profits. Some methods will not succeed on your particular blog, and that's okay. Dump them and move on, because some other methods will provide you with the profits you're looking for. Don't linger on what isn't working.

Running Multiple Blogs

Once you get your blog up and running like a top, you will want to evaluate whether or not it is producing the income you would like it to. If it is not, you will need to do some troubleshooting. If you find that your blog is running as smoothly and as profitably as it can, and it still isn't producing the profits you would like, you may have reached the upper limit of what your chosen topic can earn. If this is the case, don't fret. There are only so many blog readers available at one given time (though this number is currently skyrocketing), and that means that your chosen topic has a profit ceiling. Many of the most successful bloggers maintain blogs with limited earnings. They overcome one blog's stagnation by starting another. Running 2, 3, or 20 blogs is not uncommon in the world of professional blogging. It is much easier to create three blogs that earn $2,000 per month than it is to create one that earns $6,000. This is because each blog will have a different and large audience with untapped resources.

So if you're faced with a blog with slowing growth and slowing profits, starting a second blog may be an option. But don't be too quick to start an additional blog until you've

Beware!
Only start a second or third blog if you have the time or the resources to do so without crippling your main blog.

exhausted the possibilities of maximizing the first. Check your post quality, look for new competition, do more marketing, and then, if that doesn't work, start that second blog that you've been thinking about.

It may be necessary to begin hiring help, or soliciting the help of contributors to keep more than one blog producing reliably at the same time. Evaluate your time. Search for areas of your work day that might be easily left to somebody else. Filling that position could free you up to devote your attention elsewhere.

●　　●　　●

OK, take a deep breath. You've just read about a lot of important topics. You now know how to plan for your blog, find a blogging platform, build considerable traffic, and earn revenue from your audience. Now that most everything logistical is covered, it is time to consider the business end of things.

So go makes some notes, take another nap if you need to, and prepare for the often avoided steps to building a blogging business: becoming a business.

4

Becoming a
Business

It is time to become a fully fledged business. In order to go about business as usual, such as hiring employees, opening a business checking account, accepting credit cards with a merchant account, and so on, it is critical that you legally register your business. Also, setting up your blogging business with the government can provide you with some legal and tax protections.

Business Classifications

For tax purposes you will need to define your new blogging business to the IRS. There are several types of business classifications to choose from, each with benefits and drawbacks. Choose the one that best suits your blogging ambitions.

Sole Proprietorship

A sole proprietorship is the most common type of start-up business because it requires little paperwork. You are the only owner. Legally, financially, and tax-wise there is no difference between you and your business. Your businesss assets are your assets. Your business debt is your personal debt. And your business profits are your income.

The advantage to this type of business is that it is easy to start and you keep all the profits for yourself. You need only to file a business income form (Schedule C) along with your regular taxes. The disadvantage of this type of business is that you are personally liable for all the business's debt and mistakes. If your blog is sued for any reason, you are directly sued.

Partnership

A partnership is similar to a sole proprietorship, except instead of one proprietor, there are two. Both parties are legally and financially responsible for the business. Some partnerships are based on common interests (such as husband-wife teams) and some are based on financial need (such as the financier and the manager).

If you're interested in setting up a partnership, be sure to be excruciatingly clear going into the business about who takes on what role, who makes what decisions, and who receives what money. A clearly defined relationship will go a long way toward making the business relationship a success.

Corporation

Unlike a sole proprietorship or partnership, a corporation is its own legal entity. A corporation's debt, taxes, profits, and legal liability are separate from the corporate owner. While this provides immense protections for owners, corporations can be tricky and expensive to get started, and is therefore not often the first choice of start-up businesses. If you're interested in starting a corporation, you should contact an attorney in your area for help.

Likely you will not need to set up a corporation with the income from just one blog, though if you are considering expanding into two, four, or fourteen blogs, each with employees and considerable revenue, you may require the protections that a corporation provides.

S Corporation

An S Corporation provides tax benefits to owners. Instead of taxing owners twice like corporations do—once as corporate income tax and once on owner dividends—an S Corporation doesn't pay taxes on its corporate income. Owners only pay taxes on their own income from the S Corporation.

S Corporations also offer all the same legal and financial protections that corporations do, so this may be a smarter choice for your blogging business.

Limited Liability Corporation

Like an S Corporation, Limited Liability Corporations (LLCs) provide owners with legal and financial protection, while avoiding the double taxation that occurs in corporations. This is quickly becoming the default choice for small businesses—and a smart choice for self publishers such as bloggers. If you publish any sort of material that could be considered libelous, you should protect your personal assets by setting up an LLC.

Setting up an LLC is relatively easy as well. Talk to your local chamber of commerce or SCORE chapter about where to find the necessary forms.

Registering Your Business Name

In many states it is necessary for you to register your business name, sometimes called a "fictitious name," with the state before you can do such things as open a business bank account or apply for a bank loan. If you intend on asking your advertisers to make out their checks to

> **Tip...**
>
> **Smart Tip**
> SCORE, or the Service Corps of Retired Executives, is a volunteer organization with local branches that is dedicated to helping new businesses learn and grow. Visit www.score.org for more information.

a business name (and you should), you will be required to register that business name with the state.

Registering your business name also ensures that you have the rights to that name in your state. Other companies will still be able to operate under the same name, but if it ever came to a legal battle, you would have claim. Registration is a simple process that involves a simple form, a small processing fee, and a stamp. Check with your state's Small Business Association web site for more information.

Hiring Help

Up until this point, if you have operated your business as a sole proprietorship, you have not needed an Employer Identification Number (EIN). An EIN is to a business what a social security number is to an individual. It simply identifies your business to the IRS and will be used when you withhold income taxes from your employee's paychecks. You must receive an EIN before you begin hiring part-time or full-time employees. To apply for your EIN, you will need to fill out, and submit, IRS Form SS-4. It can be downloaded from www.irs.gov/pub/irs-pdf/fss4.pdf.

In addition to keeping your new employee's application, resume (if submitted), and references on file, you also need to collect some tax information from him or her. As the employer, you will be withholding income tax on your employee's paychecks. The amount you withhold is determined by the information your employee fills out on his or her Form W-4. You will need to keep a copy of Form W-4, and mail one to the IRS.

You must also ask your new employee to fill out Form I-9, the Employment Eligibility Verification. To do this you will need a copy of the employee's passport, or driver's license and social security card. For a complete list of acceptable forms of identification, see the back of Form I-9. You must keep every employee's Form I-9 on file for a period of three years from the hiring date. This form is not mailed to anyone.

More Protection

To further protect yourself and your blog content, we recommend registering your blog with the U.S. Copyright Office as a periodical. This will copyright your blog and your content so in the event that you find a renegade blogger

Tip...

Smart Tip
Many businesses secure an EIN number long before it is time to hire employees. In addition to its main tax purposes, it can be a handy identification number for your business if you're concerned about splashing your personal social security number about.

Smart Tip

Tip...

If you have a logo for your blog, you should consider registering it as a trademark, especially if you plan on doing any merchandising. Visit the US Patent and Trademark Office (USPTO) web site for more information at www.uspto.gov.

copying your posts, and therefore stealing your original and valuable content, you will have legal ownership of your content. If you don't have your copyright, you're without recourse.

There is a small registration fee and a few forms to fill out. After they're submitted and processed, you will receive your certificate of copyright within a quick four to five months. Find out more at www.copyright.gov/register/serial.html.

Final
Thoughts

Y ou now have the tools and the know how to start your own blogging business. Our three "P" process is now complete and you should be on your way to accomplishing your goal of establishing a professional blogging career.

Remember, blogging is a quickly evolving phenomenon. With a seemingly simple innovation it could be completely different tomorrow morning. In order for your business to keep growing, it is important for you to keep up on the changing landscape of the blogosphere. Keep reading. Keep researching. The internet in general, and blogs in particular, are great resources for keeping up-to-date on the latest developments, business models, and profit sources.

I would love to hear about the success you've had with the methods for building a profitable blogging business I've presented in this book (blogging@jsmcdougall.com). I hope you found it useful and inspirational and you are already blogging away. Blogging is an exciting development in the world. It is changing journalism and publishing while making individual creative endeavors more accessible to the world. It will be the next generation of bloggers, of which you are one, who realize blogging's full potential. I wish you luck!

Glossary

blawg (noun): A web log written by lawyers and/or concerned primarily with legal affairs.

bleg (verb): To use one's blog to beg for assistance (usually for information, occasionally for money). One who does so is a 'blegger.' Usually intended as humorous.

blogathy (noun): When you just don't give a damn about posting in your blog that day.

blogebrity (noun): A term for a person made famous through blogging. The term was coined after the eponymous internet project which was born in May of 2005.

blogorrhea (noun): An unusually high volume output of articles on a blog.

blogover (noun): A weblog redesign; done by someone other than the author or with outside consultation.

blogroll (noun): A blogroll is a collection of links to other weblogs. When present, blogrolls are often found on the front page sidebar of most weblogs.

blogstipation (noun): To be unable to think of anything to blog about, i.e. writers' block for bloggers.

blurker (pronoun): One who reads many blogs but leaves no evidence, such as comments a silent observer of blogs.

CSS (noun): An acronym for Cascading Style Sheet.

flame (verb): To flame someone is to make a hostile intemperate remark, usually of a personal nature.

instapundited (verb): To have your blog mentioned on Instapundit.com.

mediasphere (noun): The conventional media collectively (as opposed to the blogosphere). Old Media.

meme (noun): any expression (usually the smallest/shortest possible) that can convey meaning; an idea, behavior, style, or usage that spreads from person to person within a culture

moblog (noun): Moblog is a blend of the words mobile and weblog. A mobile weblog, or moblog, consists of content posted to the internet from a mobile or portable device, such as a cellular phone or PDA. Moblogs generally involve technology which allows publishing from a mobile device.

MSM: Mainstream media

permalink (noun): A link to a specific article in the archives of a blog, which will remain valid after the article is no longer listed on the blog's front page (i.e., after it has archived).

ping (noun): When used in reference to blogs, the act of sending electronic, usually automated, notice of a blog's recent update.

pingback (noun): A method for web authors to request notification when somebody links to one of their documents.

podcasting (verb): To record (usually spoken narrative) audio files (usually in MP3 format) and make them available online so that they can be downloaded and listened to rather like an 'on-demand' radio show.

post (noun): A blog or internet forum entry.

poster (noun): Someone who posts an entry to a blog.

RDF (noun): RDF is a web content syndication format. Acronym which stands for Resource Description Framework

RSS feed (noun): RSS is a family of web feed formats, specified in XML and used for web syndication.

Slashdotted (verb): To have your blog mentioned on Slashdot.org.

spambot (noun): Online code that automatically generates large numbers of unwanted messages and directs them at members of the public. Within the context of blogging, it is code which enters unsolicited comment spam.

splog (noun): Spam blog. A blog created purely as a payload target for spam. The spam itself is delivered via trackbacks, comment spamming, or e-mail and the 'splog' is where you end up if you click the spam link.

thread (noun): A series of remarks posted by people in a public comment section of a blog that follow a conversational and topic-related sequence.

trackback (noun): A mechanism for communication between blogs.

vog (noun): Video blog. A blog used to display various forms video images. Also: Vlog.

wiki (noun): a type of collaborative online software that allows readers to add content on a subject, which can also be edited by others. For example: Wikipedia.

XML (noun): A web language used for (among other things) syndication formats used on blogs. Acronym for eXtensible Markup Language

XML link (noun): Text or an image on a blog that has been linked to the blog's RSS feed.

Index

▲

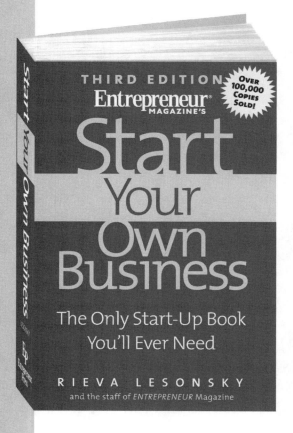